The Mahatma and the Ism

E.M.S. Namboodiripad

The Mahatma and the Ism

LeftWord

Offset edition first published in August 2010.
Reprinted April 2011.
Digital print edition, January 2020.

LeftWord Books
2254/2A Shadi Khampur
New Ranjit Nagar
New Delhi 110008
INDIA

www.leftword.com

LeftWord Books is a division of
Naya Rasta Publishers Pvt. Ltd.

ISBN 978-81-87496-98-4

Contents

EMS on Gandhi

Prakash Karat

The Mahatma and the Ism by E.M.S. Namboodiripad was the first full-fledged attempt by an Indian Marxist to evaluate the role of Gandhi in the epochal struggle for Indian independence.[1] The book was first published in January 1958. E.M.S. Namboodiripad had earlier written a series of 14 articles in *New Age*, the monthly journal of the Communist Party of India in 1955–56. EMS was at that time a member of the Polit Bureau stationed at the Party headquarters in Delhi. These articles were a review of and commentary on the monumental eight-volume biography of Gandhi by D.G. Tendulkar, *Mahatma: The Life of Mohandas Karamchand Gandhi.* These articles, along with subsequent additions and revisions, constitute the kernel of the book.

The Mahatma and the Ism remains important not just for its pioneering effort to assess Gandhism, but also for its rich content and sensitive handling of a great personality, while also subjecting the ideology and politics of that personality to incisive critical appraisal.

A few months after *Mahatma and the Ism* was published, another book appeared on Gandhi by a Communist leader. Hiren Mukherjee, the Communist parliamentarian, wrote *Gandhi: A Study.*[2] This book was wider in scope than EMS's, and dealt with Gandhi's life and political activity in greater detail, but in its

[1] S.A. Dange published a pamphlet titled *Gandhi vs Lenin* in 1921. This comparative study of the two leaders cannot be taken to be a comprehensive study of Gandhi as it was published at the beginning of the Gandhi's leadership of the national movement.

[2] Hiren Mukherjee, *Gandhi: A Study*, People's Publishing House, New Delhi, 1958.

essentials, the assessment of Gandhi by Hiren Mukherjee closely parallels that of EMS.

I

EMS was uniquely positioned to analyse the various phases of the national movement and the role of Gandhi. He began his political life as an ardent Gandhian. Throughout his life, while adhering to the Marxist world outlook, he practised many of the Gandhian principles of simplicity and personal austerity that are cherished by Indians.

EMS was one of the young Congressmen who were radicalised after the 1930–31 civil disobedience movement was withdrawn. Jawaharlal Nehru and Jayaprakash Narayan were the initial stimuli for the leftward move that led EMS to the Congress Socialist Party, of which he became one of the all-India joint secretaries. By the time EMS assumed the leadership of the Congress in Kerala in 1936, he had broken with Gandhism. In 1937, he joined the Communist Party, encouraged by the example of another former Gandhian Congressman, P. Sundarayya.

The organizational break with the Congress took place in 1939, when, under the guidance of Gandhi, the Kerala Pradesh Congress Committee, of which EMS was General Secretary, was dissolved. The All India Congress Committee disbanded the Pradesh Congress Committee, which was dominated by Left Congressmen, for its persistence in militant actions against the War.

EMS became an organizer of the Communist Party and of the peasant movement in Kerala during the period of the War. From 1943, EMS was a member of the Central Committee of the Communist Party, having been elected at its First Congress in 1943. He was also an office-bearer of the All India Kisan Sabha in the pre-independence period.

It is this experience of his work in the Congress and subsequent turn to the Communist Party that EMS drew upon when he set out to review Tendulkar's biography of Gandhi, which appeared between 1951 and 1954. That EMS himself considered this work to be of some lasting value is clear from his autobiography, *Reminiscences of an Indian Communist.*[3]

The merit of EMS's book is that it analyses the role of Gandhi in a way not done before. It does not underplay the individual role of Gandhi and the unique contribution made by him to developing the mass national movement against British rule. At the same time, it also fully takes into account the social and historical forces that shaped Gandhi and Gandhism. It sees Gandhi as a leader and his personality in the context of the class he represents; thus Gandhi as a historical figure and mass leader emerges in the context of the class relations that shaped the national movement.

Although EMS was critical of Gandhism, he did not share the early Communist sectarianism of the 1920s, which viewed Gandhi as nothing but the leader of the right-wing bourgeoisie. In that period, as EMS has pointed out elsewhere, the early Communist groups

> engaged themselves in mainly exposing the policies and programmes of the bourgeois leaders including Gandhi without participating in these struggles and sharing their bitter experience. The result was that the bourgeois leadership and the people were getting closer to each other.[4]

By contrast, EMS and a whole crop of Communists emerged subsequently from within the Congress-led national movement and went on to build the independent movement of workers and peasants and their political party.

However decisive his break from Gandhian politics, EMS, like many others of his generation, retained some Gandhian

[3] E.M.S. Namboodiripad, *Reminiscences of an Indian Communist*, National Book Centre, New Delhi, 1987.

[4] E.M.S. Namboodiripad, *A History of the Indian Freedom Struggle*, Social Scientist Press, Thiruvananthapuram, 1986.

values, which in fact became deeply ingrained in him. In 1994, that is, nearly 40 years after writing *The Mahatma and the Ism*, EMS made his last intervention on this subject. In it, he admitted that

> elements of Gandhism were by and large inherent in my lifestyle and mode of thinking even after I adopted Marxism. While expressing my ideological difference with Gandhism, I became a political activist who upheld the high values of Gandhism and tried to translate them in my personal lifestyle.[5]

II

In this book, EMS seeks to answer the question: 'How did Gandhi become the undisputed leader of the biggest national political movement of the country?' The fledgling bourgeoisie's interests initially found expression in the moderate politics of the Indian National Congress. 'Gradually, however, the class represented by them outgrew the limits set by their "moderate politics".' The main difference between Gandhi and other Congress politicians of the day was that, 'unlike the latter, Gandhi associated himself with the masses of the people, their lives, problems, sentiments and aspirations.' Through the Champaran struggle and the Ahmedabad textile workers strike, Gandhi deployed the techniques of satyagraha and hunger strike that were part of his creed of non-violent struggle. Referring to Gandhi's fast in Ahmedabad, EMS remarks:

> This was, of course, not the first time that Gandhi resorted to a fast. This, however, was the first time that he resorted to it in order to check the militancy of the fighting people.[6]

[5] E.M.S. Namboodiripad, 'Gandhian Philospophy: A Marxist Evaluation,' Sukumar Azhikode Endowment Lecture, translated from the Malayalam, University of Calicut, Kozhikode, 1994.

[6] E.M.S. Namboodiripad, *The Mahatma and the Ism*. See p. 45 below.

This significance was not lost on the rising national bourgeoisie. His success in this experiment was an

> invaluable lesson for the class of which he was the representative, the bourgeoisie. It showed them that here was a technique of struggle which could at once rally the masses and keep them away from militant actions.[7]

While highlighting the historic role played by Gandhi in drawing the masses into the national movement, EMS also points out the class mould of the first national mass movement launched under Gandhi's leadership, the non-cooperation movement in 1920:

> It will be noticed that the resolution does not suggest such forms of militant mass action as the industrial worker's general strike or peasants' struggle like non-payment of rent and seizure of land – forms of struggle which touch upon the profits of the Indian capitalists and landlords as much as the economic and political basis of the . . . rulers.[8]

The resolution stated that, for the campaign, 'a beginning should be made by the 'classes who have moulded and represented public opinion,' i.e., the bourgeoisie and the petty bourgeoisie.'

As for the Gandhian insistence on non-violent forms of struggle, EMS points out its usefulness for the bourgeoisie.

> This much talked of abhorrence of violence, however, was nothing but the bourgeoisie's natural fear that, once the working class enters the field of political action with its own weapon of struggle – the weapon of political general strike – the movement will go beyond the limits set by it.[9]

[7] Ibid.
[8] Ibid., p. 51.
[9] Ibid., p. 52.

The inflexible stand of Gandhi on Chauri Chaura stemmed from his understanding of the potential of peasant movements once unleashed. EMS points out that Chauri Chaura was not an isolated incident; it was preceded by the Moplah rebellion in Malabar, where the peasantry took to 'such typically peasant forms of revolutionary action' as the burning of landlords' records, the destruction of registry offices, attacks on government offices and distribution of food grain lying in the landlords' mansions.

Even the sympathetic account by Bhiku Parekh of Gandhi's attitude to class struggle concedes that Gandhi

> was also worried that once violence became respectable and organized, the masses would want to use it against their native exploiters, thereby dividing the nationalist movement and playing into the hands of the colonial rulers . . . He knew well that the poor were angry and frustrated . . . He was also aware of their role in the Russian and Chinese revolutions, to both of which he was a contemporary witness. He was, therefore, deeply afraid that once they were mobilised and their expectations aroused, large-scale violence was bound to result which neither he nor the Congress would be able to control.[10]

The main concern for Gandhi, according to EMS, were the consequences of an aroused peasantry. 'Once they were drawn into the movement, this new class, the peasantry, drew up its own forms of struggle and its own form of organization' (p. 30). The dread of peasant violence against landlords led Gandhi strongly to condemn the spontaneous movements of the peasantry in the 1920s. He did not allow the Congress to lead and organize peasant protests beyond a certain point and without his consent.

There have been subsequent efforts to reinterpret and reassess the role of Gandhi and his philosophy from within the Marxist

[10] Bhikhu Parekh, *Colonialism, Tradition and Reform: An Analysis of Gandhi's Political Discourse*, Sage, New Delhi, 1999, pp. 307, 318–19.

framework. One major effort was by Professor Irfan Habib in a lecture in 1995 on 'Gandhi and the National Movement.'[11] The evaluation made by Professor Habib differs from EMS's evaluation in some important respects. For Habib, Gandhi is not to be seen as a leader representing the interests of the national bourgeoisie in the national movement, but more as a 'classical modern figure'. Gandhi's approach to landlords is seen as a tactical one, followed in order to preserve the unity of the movement. Gandhi's attitude to caste, religion and social problems was that of a reformer. EMS, in his rejoinder, disagreed with some of these views.[12] While acknowledging that Marxists like Rajani Palme Dutt and himself committed 'Leftist' mistakes, he felt Habib, in trying to correct them, committed 'rightist' mistakes, overlooking the negative attributes of Gandhism.

On two counts EMS held firm to his views. First, Gandhi, as the undisputed leader of the national movement, represented the broad interests of the national bourgeoisie, which led the freedom struggle. Secondly, the Gandhian programme had no anti-landlord component with which to mobilize the peasantry, a feature of the programme that itself stemmed from a class viewpoint.

Hiren Mukherjee shared the same evaluation of Gandhian tactics and their usefulness for the bourgeoisie. In his study of Gandhism, he wrote:

> As a matter of fact, it is only fair to state that the aura of Gandhi's glory lent a certain nobility to a generally timorous bourgeois movement, which prized and utilized his capacity of mobilising the people against foreign rule and at the same time of restricting mass activity within limits thought safe for the men of property.[13]

[11] Irfan Habib, 'Gandhi and the National Movement,' *Social Scientist*, vol. 23 (4–6), April–June, 1995.

[12] E.M.S. Namboodiripad, 'For a Balanced Approach on Gandhi and the National Movement,' *Social Scientist*, vol. 23 (7–9), July–September 1995.

[13] Hiren Mukherjee, *Gandhi: A Study*, p. 200.

The programmatic demands of the Congress of the 1930 civil disobedience movement, the eleven-point charter of demands, 'once again reflected the bourgeois framework.' EMS noted that they did 'not include anything which the workers or peasants demand from their employers, landlords or usurers. The only demand which is of direct interest to the peasants is the 50 per cent reduction on land revenue' (p. 53). A corollary to this was the appearance of demands in the interests of the Indian capitalists. B.T. Ranadive, dissecting the charter, recorded that Gandhi, who in the 1920s considered modern industry sinful, had now demanded protection for Indian textile industries. 'By now Gandhism had shed its earlier anti-West trappings and was openly advocating the immediate demands of the national capitalist class.'[14]

The standpoint of EMS on the pro-landlord component of Gandhism reflected the experience of all Left Congressmen who later became Communists. P. Ramamurti, who was an active CSP leader and who become one of the founding leaders of the Communist Party in Tamil Nadu, noted the phenomenon of the Congress party becoming a party of the bourgeoisie and landlords in the 1930s. He observed that while the statutory landlords such as the zamindars and inamdars were overwhelmingly pro-British, other sections of landlords joined the Congress. According to him:

> . . . under Gandhi's leadership, the Congress assured the landlords that they would not be affected. In the Bardoli resolution and during the non-cooperation movement, the Congress had assured landlords that it did not stand for the cessation of rent payment to the landlords . . . The point I want to stress is that, by 1930, the Congress had emerged as the representative of capitalists *and* landlords; it had acquired the character of a bourgeois-landlord party.[15]

[14] B.T. Ranadive, (1986), 'India's Freedom Struggle,' *Social Scientist*, vol. 14 (159–60), August–September 1986, p. 118.

[15] V.K. Ramachandran, 'Conversations with Comrade P. Ramamurti, 1982–84,' *CPI (M) XIX Congress Souvenir*, Coimbatore, 2008.

In an evaluation of the legacy of Gandhi, P.C. Joshi, General Secretary of the CPI from 1935 to 1946 and perhaps the firmest advocate of Congress-Communist unity, could not help observing that

> The Mahatma resisted more successfully the independent class organizations of the peasantry. We of the Left tried our best to set them up and they grew in areas where the Left was strong, but after independence, following the disruption of the national democratic movement and Left unity, they became local islands.[16]

While both EMS and Irfan Habib acknowledge that it was Gandhi who could identify with the peasant masses and speak the idiom and language that helped in drawing them in to the national movement, EMS was consistent in holding that Gandhism hampered the development of a powerful agrarian movement against feudalism and landlordism.

It is relevant to see how Gandhi's use of the religious idiom and language aroused the peasant masses to join the independence struggle. Talking about Tolstoy, one of the ideological mentors of Gandhi, Lenin had said:

> Tolstoy's doctrine is certainly utopian and in content is reactionary in the most precise and most profound sense of the word. But that certainly does not mean that the doctrine . . . did not contain critical elements capable of providing valuable material for the enlightenment of the advanced classes.[17]

When commenting on Gandhian philosophy and politics, EMS noted their utopian and socially conservative features, but

[16] P.C. Joshi, 'The Legacy', *Seminar*, No. 122, p. 26.

[17] V.I. Lenin, 'Lev Tolstoi and His Epoch,' *Collected Works*, vol. 17, Progress Publishers, Moscow, p. 52.

did not fail to recognize the appeal that they had for the rural masses, who were roused to action for a better future:

> It may appear self-contradictory if one were to say that Gandhi with his 'reactionary' social outlook was instrumental in bringing about a profoundly revolutionary phenomenon – the drawing of the mass of the rural poor into the arena of the modern national-democratic movement. This self-contradiction, however, is a manifestation of the contradiction in the real political life of our nation, arising out of the fact that the national-democratic movement was led by the bourgeoisie, linked with feudalism.[18]

The other issue on which EMS and Habib differed was the role of the different strands within the national movement. For EMS, the crucial aspect of the relationship of the working-class movement with the bourgeois-led national movement was that the former joined the united front against imperialism while maintaining its ideological and political independence. It was always from this standpoint that EMS strove to delineate how the fledgling communist party sought independently to mobilize workers and peasants on an anti-imperialist and anti-feudal agenda and draw them into the independence struggle.

Thus, while Irfan Habib is right in stating that there was only one national movement, EMS emphasized that, within this movement, there was a separate strand of the Left, which sought to organize the workers and peasants on a class basis and develop their political platform independently. In class terms EMS delineated three strands in the freedom movement: the bourgeois, the radical petty bourgeois and the working class strands. There is no doubt that the first strand became the dominant and hegemonic influence – a development that owed a lot to Gandhi's vision and leadership.

[18] E.M.S. Namboodiripad, *The Mahatma and the Ism*. See pp. 151–52 below.

III

The critique of Gandhism by EMS includes a strong appreciation of the courageous and noble fight that Gandhi conducted in the final period of his life. His non-acceptance of the Partition, his valiant efforts to douse communal fires by staying at Noakhali and his last fast demanding that Pakistan be given the Rs. 55 crore due to it from the Indian government, all put him on a plane different from other Congress leaders, who were more concerned with sharing the spoils of office than anything else.

There is a need to reassess the secular heritage left behind by Gandhi. Communists are uneasy with the Gandhian use of the religious idiom; with, for instance the harking back to *sanatana dharma*, and his exhortation to the people to fight for *Ram rajya*. EMS was thus critical of the anti-modernist stance of Gandhi as set out in *Hind Swaraj*, and considered Gandhi's views on modern medicine, science and technology as obscurantist. However, while deeply appreciating Gandhi's resolute fight against communalism during his last days, the book does not take into account adequately the secular aspects of Gandhi's outlook.

Gandhi was consistent in his stand that all religions be equally respected and all religious communities be treated equally. He also spoke about the need for a secular state in India and was of the view that religion and the state should be separate. He was against proposed state funding for the renovation of the Somnath temple.[19]

The Gandhi-Nehru legacy has been the mainstay of Indian secularism, however flawed it may be. The effort by the RSS to appropriate Gandhi and disembowel his inherently secular outlook by incorporating his religious world-view within the ambit of Hindutva is a diabolic move by the very forces who considered Gandhi anathema and who were instrumental in his death at the hands of a Hindu fanatic.

Whatever political differences the Communists had with the

[19] Anil Nauriya, 'Gandhi on Secular Law and State,' *The Hindu*, October 22, 2003.

Mahatma, his assassination was deeply mourned by the Communists of EMS's generation. One of the last public acts of P. Krishna Pillai, legendary founder-member of the Communist movement in Kerala, just before he went underground and subsequently died of a snake-bite, was to lead a rally in Kottayam to protest Gandhi's killing. This was in contrast to the celebrations by the Hindutvawadis, an act that Nehru summed up thus: 'The evil has not ended with the killing of Gandhi. It was an even more shameful thing for some people to celebrate this killing in various ways.'[20]

EMS captures the idealism, the grandeur and the tragedy of the last days of Gandhi. The book seeks to answer the question of how Gandhi rapidly became a prophet outcast. In the days when the masses had to be mobilized to fight British imperialism, Gandhian methods, particularly the technique of non-violent resistance, were found useful by the bourgeoisie. 'However, once the struggle against imperialism was crowned with success in the sense that the bourgeoisie and its class allies got state power, [Gandhism] proved a hindrance to the self-interest of the bourgeoisie.' EMS points out that Gandhi remained true to his values. The new rulers rejected his views on the question of Hindu-Muslim unity and on the need for the dissolution, on account of its corruption, of the Congress Party.

While EMS remained consistent in his views on Gandhism till the end, he continued to hold that there were possibilities for joint action by Marxists and Gandhians, a fact that is mentioned at the end of the book. With the menacing growth of the Hindutva forces, the Gandhian heritage must be protected from the saffron efforts to appropriate it. Though enfeebled and institutionalized by official patronage, there are some in the Gandhian stream who are ranged against the processes of liberalization and privatization ushered in during the nineties. When the ruling classes have firmly

[20] Jawaharlal Nehru, 'Two Weeks of Sorrow and Searching' (1948), in S. Gopal and Uma Iyengar (eds.), *The Essential Writings of Jawaharlal Nehru*, vol. 1, Oxford University Press, New Delhi, 2003.

turned their backs on the concepts dear to Gandhi, such as swaraj, swadeshi and ahimsa, what is required is the preservation of what is valuable in Gandhi's thought and practice in terms of the people's and national sovereignty. The exercise begun by E.M.S. Namboodiripad in the early fifties of a critical appraisal of Gandhi and his ism, is not over. It needs to be carried forward. Gandhism must be rescued from both the mummified official version and the pernicious efforts to distort and appropriate it for communal purposes.

Preface to the Second Edition

The first fourteen chapters of this volume had originally been serialized in the *New Age* monthly in 1955–56. After necessary revisions and additions, they were brought out in book form in January 1958. A second edition was subsequently brought out with no changes in the text but with the addition of an introductory note by the author.

The present edition has dispensed with the introductory note carried in the second edition but has added a final chapter briefly reviewing the developments of the last 23 years. As regards the text, some minor revisions have been made – mainly of an additional nature.

This edition is being brought out, since the earlier ones have, for several years, been out of stock and there is persistent demand from those interested in the subject. I take this opportunity to thank the publishers for having brought out this volume.

New Delhi
March 25, 1981

E.M.S. Namboodiripad

Introductory

Time was when even eminent Gandhians like Dr. J.C. Kumarappa and Pandit Sunderlal did not escape from being denounced as 'communist fellow-travellers' for merely telling the truth about the Soviet Union and China, of the remarkable progress that these countries have made in bettering human relations and providing a decent living standard to their peoples. Genuine Gandhians that they are, they could not help speaking out that what was happening in these countries was 'Gandhism in action.'

Those were days when the then Madras chief minister, Shri C. Rajagopalachari, had declared war on the communists, whom he described as his 'enemy number one.' Those were days when the then railway minister banned the sale of Soviet books and magazines at railway bookstalls as 'tendentious' literature while, at the same time, permitting the free circulation of all the decadent and pornographic stuff imported from the 'free world.' Those were days when the then commerce minister stood up on the floor of the parliament and opposed the resolution moved by communist MP Sundarayya, advocating trade agreements with the Soviet Union.

Much water has since flown down the Ganga as well as the Volga. In less than a year after the commerce minister's opposition to the communist resolution on Indo-Soviet trade relations, the Indo-Soviet agreement was signed. Innumerable delegations from the two countries have visited each other—cultural delegations, delegations of technicians of various types, of parliamentary and political leaders, delegations of representatives of mass organizations, etc. The very Rajagopalachari who declared the communists to be his 'enemy number one' has made some of the most forthright statements praising the Soviet Union's role in the struggle for peace and its attitude towards the banning of atomic and hydrogen weapons. Above all, the unprecedentedly warm and enthusiastic welcome accorded to our prime minister in the Soviet Union, followed by a similar welcome accorded to the Soviet leaders in out country, has made the air reverberate with the inspiring slogan, 'Hindi-Russi Bhai-Bhai.'

These friendly relations between the two countries have become possible because the leaders of both have accepted 'peaceful coexistence of states following different social systems' as the basis of international relations. As Sriman Narayan, general secretary of the Congress, wrote:

> We have not the slightest intention of interfering with the ideologies of other countries, nor can we afford to allow any other country to interfere with our way of life. (*AICC Economic Review*, 1 December 1955)

Both the Indian and Soviet leaders have, at the same time, pointed out that the social and state systems existing in the two countries, and the philosophical outlook guiding their governmental leaders, are different from each other. Bulganin and Khrushchov combined their warm call for mutual cooperation between the governments and peoples of the two countries in the cause of peace with a spirited defence of the philosophy and practice of Marxism. The leaders of the ruling party in out country, in their turn, have also made it clear that they stick to the philosophy and practice of what is generally referred to as Gandhism. One of them, Sriman Narayan, declared unequivocally:

> It must always be remembered that the means or methods employed for the achievement of these objectives (world peace and cooperation on the basis of the Five Principles and improvement of the economic lot of the common man by eliminating exploitation and bringing about economic justice) are fundamentally different in India and in the Soviet Union. . . . *There can be no compromise between the ideologies of Lenin and Gandhi.* (Ibid., emphasis added.)

This makes it clear that while enormous possibilities have opened out for mutual cooperation between India and the Soviet Union in the field of foreign relations—beneficial to the peoples of both countries, as well as to the cause of peace in the world—the internal struggle between the ruling party in our country (which claims to base itself on the teachings of Gandhism) and those parties of the democratic opposition (which claim to base themselves on Marxism-Leninism) will continue unabated. Peaceful coexistence between *states* and cooperation between them for purposes of solving *international problems* does not resolve *conflicts between different classes inside our country* which find expression in different ideologies. For example, the unity of the Indian people that was magnificently shown in the warm welcome given to the Soviet leaders has not resolved such questions of internal policy as:

1. Can the land problem in our country be solved through the Bhoodan movement, or does it require the development of an organized peasant movement strong enough to smash the power of the landlords and other reactionary classes?
2. Can the programme of rapid industrialization (to which the whole country is now committed) be brought about on the basis of compromise with, or determined struggles against, foreign monopoly capital?
3. Is the objective of rapid industrialization itself a correct objective, or, does it come into conflict with the Sarvodaya ideal to which the leaders of the ruling party seem to be committed?

Differences and conflicts continue on these issues not only between Gandhism and Marxism-Leninism, but even between various trends claiming to base themselves on Gandhism.

It has become necessary under these circumstances that Marxist-Leninists try to make a correct appraisal of the philosophy and practice of Gandhism. Such an examination has been facilitated by the appearance of the eight-volume biography

Mahatma, by D.G. Tendulkar. In this the author claims to have tried 'to tell the story faithfully and, as far as possible, in the words of Gandhi himself, who not only took the leading part in the movement but wrote the best commentary on it' (I, pp. xvii–xviii).

After collecting material on his life, the author had it checked by Gandhi himself.

> When I met him last on 22 January 1948, we discussed the smallest details—the format of the biography, type, illustrations, standardization of spelling, quotation marks and even hyphens. He took great interest in my work and always gave me his gracious cooperation (I, pp. xviii–xix).

The author also acknowledges the help and cooperation which he received from numerous followers and disciples of the Mahatma, including Mahadev Desai, R.R. Diwakar and K.G. Mashruwala. Above all, the book carries a highly appreciative foreword by the prime minister who considers 'this book to be of great value as a record, not only of the life of a man supreme in his generation, but also of a period of India's history which has intrinsic importance of its own' (I, p. xiv).

Early years

Appropriately enough, Tendulkar begins the first volume with a twenty-five page account of our history—from 'Plassey to Amritsar.' He present great events and personalities—the revolt of 1857 which 'brought forth among others the inspiring figure of Rani Lakshmibai of Jhansi who died fighting on the battlefield'; the famines which enveloped India under British rule, beginning with the Bengal famine of 1770; the great Ram Mohun Roy, who insisted on visiting a French ship as a mark of homage from his motherland to France which had raised aloft the banner of revolution for liberty, equality, fraternity; scholar-politicians like Pherozshah Mehta, Dadabhai Naoroji, Ranade, Tilak and a host of others; the inspiring scene at the Amsterdam session of the International Socialist Congress in 1904 at which the Grand Old Man of Indian nationalism, Dadabhai Naoroji, represented the people of India and 'the delegates leapt to their feet and stood uncovered before him in solemn silence to mark their respect for India's representative'; the call of Swaraj from the platform of the Indian National Congress; the appearance of the new radical school of politics led by the well-known trio: Lal, Bal, Pal (Lala Lajpat Rai, Bal Gangadhar Tilak and Bipin Chandra Pal); the historic trial and the barbaric sentence on Tilak against which there was nationwide protest, including a protest strike by the textile workers of Bombay, probably the first political strike of workers in India, hailed immediately by Lenin; the new upsurge of anti-imperialism which emerged in the period of, and immediately after, the First World War, etc.

It was in such an epoch, an epoch in which the Indian people were slowly getting unified in and through the anti-imperialist struggle, that Mohandas Karamchand Gandhi was born as the last son of Karamchand Gandhi. Uttamchand, the grandfather, as well as Karamchand, the father of Mohandas, had been prime ministers on several Kathiawad States.

> In this service, they had acquired a reputation for loyalty, ability and character, rare qualities in State officials. . . . The Gandhi clan played an important part in the political life of Porbandar (I pp. 27–8).

The impact of the epoch seems to have been felt by young Mohandas. We are told that the argument in favour of meat-eating which most appealed to him was, 'Behold the mighty Englishman! He rules the Indian small; because, being a meat-eater, he is five cubits tall!'—the popular doggerel among schoolboys in those days. 'If the country took to meat-eating,' thought Mohandas, 'the English can be overcome.' This, of course, was a brief interlude in the otherwise vegetarian life which the Mahatma led for nearly 80 years.

We are also told that, from very early boyhood, Mohandas used to argue with his mother that untouchability was not sanctioned by religion. Mohandas had also to face ostracism from his caste for going abroad for his studies. 'This boy,' said a general meeting of the caste, 'shall be treated as an outcaste from today. Whoever helps him, or goes to see him off at the dock, shall be punishable with a fine of one rupee and four annas.'

One of the letters of introduction which young Mohandas carried to England was addressed to Dadabhai Naoroji.

> Dadabhai was in London at the time. In 1890 he started *India*, a journal for the discussion of Indian affairs, which influenced the young Indian students in England. . . . (He) used to address meetings at the Indian Association. Gandhi once mustered courage at one of these meetings to present to Dadabhai the note of introduction. Dadabhai said, 'you can come and have my advice whenever you like' (I, p. 37).

In London, Mohandas Gandhi, the budding lawyer, tried to

interest himself in various progressive movements. Though he was not an atheist, he got interested in atheism through Charles Bradlaugh, then its chief British advocate. Along with several British celebrities, Gandhi attended the funeral of Bradlaugh. '"For atheists like Bradlaugh, truth held the same place as God for others," was the opinion of Gandhi.'

It is interesting to note that, during the London dockers' strike in 1889, Gandhi in the company of an Indian friend went to Cardinal Manning to congratulate him for helping the strikers.

However, it is characteristic of the future Mahatma that the movement which interested him most while in London was—*vegetarianism*!

> In one of his wanderings in the town in search of vegetarian dishes, Gandhi came across a queer restaurant which not only served vegetarian diet but propagated it through literature. He bought here *Salt's Plea for Vegetarianism* which created in him an interest in dietetics. He came in contact with those who were regarded as pillars of vegetarianism . . . . He joined the London Vegetarian Society and soon found himself on its executive committee. He helped to design its badge. Full of zeal, he started a vegetarian club in his locality, Bayswater. He became its secretary . . . . He contributed nine articles on Hindu customs and diet to the magazine, *Vegetarian* (I, pp. 35–6).

All this in an epoch and in a country which the author of *Mahatma* describes as follows:

> New ideas were preached and practiced as never before or after in the history of England. The Independent Labour Party was formed in 1887. The Fabian Society under the leadership of Sydney Webb and Bernard Shaw was popularizing socialism and scientific thought. The first volume of *Das Kapital* by Karl Marx had just appeared in England in 1887 and was accepted as the Bible of the working

> class. Marx's colleague, Friedrich Engels, who was living in England, brought out the second volume in German in 1885 and was now working on the third volume of *Das Kapital.* In 1889, *Fabian Essays* was published by Bernard Shaw. Darwin's epoch-making *Descent of Man* which had been published in 1871 was being discussed. Kropotkin's *Mutual Aid* was appearing in the *Nineteenth Century* and Kropotkin himself was propagating his ideas in England. Ruskin and William Morris created new interest in the art world (I, p. 3).

The man who preferred the movement for vegetarianism to all these radical, intellectual and practical-political movements would have appeared to many at the time as crankish. Future developments, however, showed that there was nothing crankish about it. His veneration for the Grand Old Man of India (Dadabhai Naoroji); his sincere respect for, but differences with, the British atheist and friend of India, Charles Bradlaugh; his interest in the strike of London dockers; his identification with the vegetarian movement—all these were part of a philosophy of action which was to be decisive in the history of India for the next half century.

This was, as a matter of fact, revealed in the next few years, years in which the young barrister, Mohandas Gandhi, practised both his law and his philosophy of life in relation to the practical living conditions of Indians in South Africa. Tendulkar takes us, in more than 130 pages, through the years 1893 to 1914, in the course of which Gandhi perfected his technique of satyagraha, to be tried subsequently on a nationwide scale in India in 1921, 1930, 1932 and 1942. In the later movements, Gandhi did, of course, further develop and perfect the technique of satyagraha. But, in this very first experiment are to be seen the main outline of the philosophy and practice of what has now come to be known as Gandhism. It will, therefore, be useful for us here to note the distinguishing features of the movement in South Africa as it developed in the course of two decades.

Firstly, the South African Indian movement was, as were the movements of other sections abroad, *an all-class movement*,—the issue being one which affected Indians of all classes and creeds—the issue of equal rights for Indians with Europeans. For instance, when Gandhi drew up the petition requesting the South African assembly to postpone further discussion of the Bill disfranchising Indians.

> Young people who never before had done any public work were drawn into the work. For the first time, a good number of Christian youths were brought together. The volunteers with knowledge of English and several others sat up the whole night to make copies of the petition. Merchant volunteers went out in their own carriages to obtain signatures (I, p. 49).

Not only was this the case in South Africa, it was so in India as well. When Gandhi came to India for a short while in 1896, he popularized the cause of Indians in South Africa and received good response from the newspapers and politicians in India. Even Anglo-Indian papers like the *Pioneer* and *The Times of India* commented favourably on the pamphlet which Gandhi wrote on the subject.

As the South African movement developed, Gandhi began to receive financial help from the richest sections of Indian society. Among the donors for the satyagraha fund in South Africa were to be found such names as the founder of the House of Tatas, Ratanji Jamshedji Tata, who gave Rs. 25,000; the Aga Khan, who collected Rs. 3,000 at the 1909 session of the All India Muslim League; J.B. Petit, who remitted £ 400 and the Nizam of Hyderabad who donated Rs. 2,500.

Secondly, though the movement was thus one which secured the blessings of the richest sections of Indian society, it *drew its real strength from the militancy and self-sacrificing spirit of the poor toiling sections of Indians in South Africa*. This was natural because, while disabilities like disfranchisement affected all classes of Indians, it was the poor indentured labourers who had to face the worst forms of oppression and exploitation. The first experience which Gandhi had of the life of indentured labourers is described as follows by the author:

> A Tamil man in tattered clothes, head-gear in hand, with two front teeth broken and his mouth bleeding stood before the young barrister. Gandhi was shocked to see this spectacle and persuaded him to put his turban on and behave like an equal. It was a new experience to the poor slave. Balasundaram, as this poor visitor was called, was serving his indenture under a well-known European resident of Durban. His master beat the helpless worker till he bled. Gandhi sent for a doctor to secure a certificate and took the injured man to a magistrate. It was not Gandhi's desire to get the employer punished but he wanted Balasundaram to be released from him. Like the slave, the indentured labourer was the property of his master. Gandhi succeeded in transferring him to someone else. Balasundaram's case reached the ears of every indentured labourer as far as Madras, and Gandhi came to be regarded as their friend (I, p. 52).

Once aroused and drawn into action, the poor indentured labourers displayed such marvels of heroism which the working class alone is capable of showing. In a chapter entitled 'The Epic March,' the author describes how six thousand coal-mine workers of Newcastle (South Africa) went on a strike which became an inseparable part of the struggle. In the course of this struggle, they showed heroism and capacity for organization.

> The strike was in full swing and the stream of labourers still continued by rail and road. Two women with grim courage reached Charlestown though their little ones died on the way. One of the children died due to exposure on the march and the other fell down from the arms of its mother while she was crossing the stream and was drowned. But the brave mothers refused to be dejected and one of them said: 'We

> must not pine for the dead who will not come back to us for all our pining. It is the living for whom we must work' (I, p. 170).

Gandhi was greatly moved by this spirit of struggle and self-sacrifice shown by the common people and it left an indelible impression on his mind. We find, for example, the following remarks in his reply to the address of welcome which he and his wife received in Madras in 1915:

> If one-tenth of the language that has been used in this address is deserved by us, what language do you propose to use for those who lost their lives, and, therefore, finished their work, on behalf of your suffering countrymen in South Africa? What language do you propose to use for Nagappan, Narayanaswamy, lads of seventeen or eighteen years, who braved in simple faith all the trials, all the sufferings, and all the indignities for the sake of the honour of the motherland? What language do you propose to use with reference to Valliamma, a sweet girl of sixteen years, who was discharged from Martizburg prison, skin and bone, suffering from fever to which she succumbed after about a month's time? You have said that I inspired those great men and women, but I cannot accept that proposition. It was they, the simple-minded folk, who worked away in faith, never expecting the slightest reward, who inspired me to the proper level, and who compelled me by their great sacrifice, by their great faith, by their great trust in the great God to do the work that I was able to do. It is my misfortune that I and my wife have been obliged to work in the limelight and you have magnified out of all proportions this little work we have been able to do. They deserve the crown which you would seek to impose upon us. These young men deserve all the adjectives that you have so affectionately, but blindly, lavished upon us (I, pp. 200–1).

Thirdly, though the struggle was one in which *the working people played the most heroic and, therefore, the most decisive role, it was not they but Gandhi who decided the course which the movement should take.* From the beginning to the end of the struggle in South Africa, as in the case of subsequent struggles which the Mahatma led, we discover a familiar and common characteristic: the great mass of the people show marvels of heroism and sacrifice, but a few leaders at the top plan and direct the movement along the path which they think best. As a matter of fact, we can perceive, in general outline, all the elements of the technique of organization and struggle which Gandhi adopted in later years.

The starting and conducting of a paper, *The Indian Opinion*, the forerunner of *Young India* and *Harijan*; the organization of the Phoenix Settlement in 1904 and of the Tolstoy Farm in 1910, the forerunners of the Sabarmati and Wardha ashrams; the minutely worked out rules of conduct for the inmates of the settlements and of the observance of self-imposed 'discipline,' as the essential pre-condition for starting and conducting struggles; the scrupulously worded correspondence with the authorities before and during struggles; correspondence and negotiations even from inside jail; the settlements arrived at with the authorities without the knowledge or consent of the mass of the people who participated in the struggle; the personal guidance given by Gandhi himself, even on the minutest details of the struggle, followed by the appointment of his successor when he is arrested—all these features of the manner of preparing, conducting and calling off struggles appeared for the first time in South Africa.

One remarkable thing in this connection is the extremely reactionary *social outlook* which guided Gandhi throughout his activities. It is here that we find the real significance of his membership of the Vegetarian Association while in England. For, just as he integrated his vegetarianism, his sense of solidarity with the striking dockers of London and total indifference, if not contempt, for the radical thinking of those days; similarly, in South Africa, he integrated the militant struggles of the common people with an obscurantist ideology. What is worse, at the very time when he was leading these militant struggles, we find him taking these very obscurantist ideas to the common people. Thus he stands in marked contrast to Marx, Engels and Lenin—the last, by the way, a contemporary of his. While Gandhi, the young barrister, was writing articles for the *Vegetarian*, Lenin, also a young lawyer, was translating Marx, Sydney Webb, etc., and himself writing *The Development of Capitalism in Russia.* Lenin combined the militant mass movement of the working class with the most advanced ideology; Gandhi combined it with the most reactionary and obscurantist of ideologies that was current in the contemporary world.

See, for example, how he formulates his outlook on the modern world in his *Hind Swaraj* or *Indian Home Rule* in 1909. As Tendulkar himself sums up, *Hind Swaraj* is a severe condemnation of 'modern civilization.' It is divided into twenty chapters, dealing with Swaraj, civilization, lawyers, doctors, machinery, education, passive resistance and other matters. Gandhi himself summarized the contents of the book in a letter to a friend which Tendulkar quotes in full. The following extracts from it will show Gandhi's world outlook:

> . . . It is not the British people who are ruling India but it is modern civilization, through its railways, telegraph, telephone, and almost every invention which has been claimed to be a triumph of civilization. Bombay, Calcutta, and the other chief cities of India are the real plague-spots. If British rule were replaced tomorrow by Indian rule based on modern methods, India would be no better off, except that she would be able to retain some of the money that is drained away to England; but then India would only become a second or fifth nation of Europe or America. . . . Medical science is the concentrated essence of black magic. Quackery is infinitely preferable to what passes for high medical skill as such. Hospitals are the instruments that the Devil has been

> using for his own purpose, in order to keep his hold on his kingdom. They perpetuate vice, misery and degradation and real slavery. . . . If there were no hospitals for venereal diseases, or even for consumptives, we should have less consumption, and less sexual vice amongst us. India's salvation consists in unlearning what she has learnt during the past fifty years or so. The railways, telegraphs, hospitals, lawyers, doctors and such like have all to go (I, p. 130).

Not only did Gandhi preach these ideas, but he tried to practise them in organizing his followers in the Phoenix Settlement, in the Tolstoy Farm and at all times of struggle. He tried to bring up boys and girls, who were taken as inmates of the Settlement and the Farm, on the lines of what was subsequently perfected in the well-known Vows and Truth—*ahimsa*, celibacy, non-stealing, non-possession and control of the palate. Having the utmost contempt for the ideological and intellectual moulding of the young generation, he tried to substitute uncritical faith for independent thinking.

In all this, however, there is something which appeals to the idealism, selflessness and spirit of sacrifice of the boys and girls who flocked to his banner. Conceding the obscurantist content of his social outlook was the idealist willingness to undergo suffering in struggle against evil. All the contempt that Gandhi had for modern civilization, the contempt which he tried to inculcate in his disciples, had taken the form of opposition to imperialist exploitation of the Indian and other oppressed peoples. The following description of petty-bourgeois socialism given by the founders of historical materialism in their well-known work, *Manifesto of the Communist Party*, may be said to be true to a certain extent of Gandhi's *Hind Swaraj*:

> This school of socialism dissected with great acuteness the contradictions in the conditions of modern production. It laid bare the hypocritical apologies of economists. It proved,

> incontrovertibly, the disastrous effects of machinery and division of labour; the concentration of capital and land in a few hands; over-production and crises; it pointed out the inevitable ruin of the petty bourgeois and peasant, the misery of the proletariat, the anarchy in production, the crying inequalities in the distribution of wealth, the industrial war of extermination between nations, the dissolution of old moral bonds, of the old family relations, of the old nationalities (K. Marx and F. Engels, *Selected Works*, Vol. I, p. 57).

Gandhi's critique of modern civilization, however, had nothing to do with the anti-imperialism of the oppressed peoples. It is remarkable how, at the very time when he was thundering against 'modern civilization,' he was acting as a loyal subject of the British Empire, which was at that time one of the biggest centres of that civilization. As he himself subsequently put it in his well-known letter 'To Every Englishman in India':

> I put my life in peril four times for the cause of the empire—at the time of the Boer War when I was in charge of the ambulance corps, whose work was mentioned in General Buller's dispatches, at the time of the Zulu revolt in Natal when I was in charge of a similar corps, at the time of the commencement of the late war when I raised an ambulance corps and as a result of the strenuous training had a severe attack of pleurisy, and, lastly, in fulfillment of my promise to Lord Chelmsford at the War Conference in Delhi, I threw myself in such an active recruiting campaign in Kheda district, involving long and trying marches, that I had an attack of dysentery which proved almost fatal. I did all these in the belief that acts such as mine must gain for my country an equal status in the empire (II, pp. 30–1).

All this at a time when a new spirit was emerging in the

country—the spirit of revolt against imperialism. Characteristic of Gandhi and his philosophy of non-violence is that, while on the one hand, he was serving the Empire by recruiting young men as cannon-fodder for imperialism's wars, he was one of the few, even in England, to denounce Madanlal Dhingra, who attempted to assassinate Sir Curzon Wylie. At the police court, Dhingra claimed that it was his right as a patriot to do this deed:

> I believe that a nation held down by foreign bayonets is in a perpetual state of war, since often battle is rendered impossible to a disarmed race.... Poor in wealth and intellect, a son like myself has nothing else to offer to the mother but his own blood, and so I have sacrificed the same on her alter. The lesson required in India at present is to learn how to die, and the only way to teach it is by dying ourselves. Therefore, I die, and glory in my martyrdom (I, p. 125).

This statement of Dhingra drew from the mouth of the arch-imperialist Winston Churchill, then under-secretary for the colonies, the remark, 'the finest ever made in the name of patriotism.' But Gandhi had something else to say on that. 'Those who believe that India has gained by Dhingra's act and other similar acts in India make a serious mistake. Dhingra was a patriot, but his love was blind. He gave his body in a wrong way, its result can only be mischievous.'

Here, therefore, we see a man who rouses large masses of the common people in action against imperialist exploitation and oppression; who stands at the head of those hundreds of men and women who leave their impress on history by the heroism and self-sacrificing spirit shown in the course of struggle; who, therefore, secures the allegiance and confidence of thousands of people throughout India; who, however, tries his best to convince his followers that the way to end exploitation is not militant struggle against it, but serving its war and oppression; who denounces the patriotic acts of revolutionaries like Dhingra in the name of non-violence but has no qualms of conscience in sending scores of people to their death as imperialism's cannon-fodder; who, above all, in the name of opposing imperialist exploitation, denounces all that is modern, scientific and progressive in human civilization.

Non-Cooperation

It was such a man who entered the scene of India's national politics towards the end of the First World War—a man who was undoubtedly respected by such venerable national leaders as Gokhale, but considered rather 'crankish' in various ways. Tendulkar tells us, for example, that Gokhale and his colleagues in the Servants of India Society had great respect and love for him, yet he was not accepted as a member of the Society because, in Gokhale's own words, 'they are hesitating to take any risk, lest their high regard for you should be jeopardized.' He also narrates how Gokhale was amused, if not shocked, when Gandhi told him about his decision of making a tour of India, travelling third class, in order that he might acquaint himself with the wretched condition of the lower class passengers.

Yet, a few years after he came to India and settled down, he became the undisputed leader of the biggest national-political movement which our country had witnessed. There were probably very few who were at one with him in his social and philosophical outlook; most of his elders and equals in the political movement had ideas very different from his on everything in relation to personal life as well as politics. Yet, hardly had he entered the scene of national politics than they became spellbound by his personality and came under his political and even personal influence and submitted themselves to his advice and guidance. Men and women, towering far above him in intellectual capacity, virtually pledged themselves to service under his guidance, and even subordinated their judgements to his.

This is, on the face of it, an amazing phenomenon. But perhaps, it is not so amazing after all. For, all that was out of the ordinary, religious and spiritualistic in Gandhi's social outlook, all that was unique in the tactics which he pursued in order to realize his political aims and objectives, had one peculiar quality—they were all perfectly suited to the requirements of a class that was daily growing in Indian society and was increasingly asserting itself in the country's national-political life.

It will be useful, in this connection, to remind ourselves that, as early as in the first half of the 19th century, symptoms of the rise of a new class had appeared in Indian society. The growth of a movement for progressive social reforms—reforms in the field of marriage, women's rights, inheritance, etc.—as well as a movement for the development of a new culture—represented by Raja Ram Mohun Roy and his prototypes in the various provinces of India—showed that the middle class of the pre-British days was slowly acquiring the characteristic features of a modern bourgeoisie. Fostered as it was by the new rulers—the British—this class was so loyal to the British regime that it wanted a replica of English civilization to be built in India and, to that extent, came into conflict with the British, who looked upon bourgeois political democracy as an article strictly for internal consumption and not for export. It was this dual character of the rising bourgeoisie that was reflected in the 'moderate politics' of the pioneers of the Indian National Congress.

Gradually, however, the class represented by them outgrew the limits set by their moderate politics.' The steady growth of the bourgeois intelligentsia, the slow but sure growth in the economic power of the commercial and industrial bourgeoisie, the experience which both of them gathered during the several decades of their attempt to modernize India, and above all, the new stirrings of the democratic movement in such oriental countries as Japan and China as well as the Russian revolution of 1905, led to the emergence of what was then known as 'extremist politics.' As opposed to the old school of leaders like Gokhale, Naoroji and others, emerged a new school represented by Tilak and others. As opposed to the time-honoured practice of passing resolutions, leading deputations and such other methods of 'loyalist' agitation, a new form of popular agitation began to emerge. This new form became so powerful in rallying the people against the British regime as to throw the rulers into utter panic.

It was this new form of popular agitation that endeared the new generation of leaders like the well-known trio of Lala Lajpat Rai, Bal Gangadhar Tilak, Bipin Chandra Pal among the people and made Tilak the first hero of the modern national movement when he was convicted to six years of imprisonment. It was this that roused the entire country on the issue of the partition of Bengal and gave rise to the movement of Swadeshi—the first nationwide movement for the economic emancipation of the country. It was, again, under the impact of these new stirrings that what has incorrectly been called the 'terrorist' movement of Bengal, Punjab, UP, etc., came into existence, led by such revolutionary groups as the Anusilan and Yugantar in Bengal, and the Gaddar in the Punjab.

The conflict between the old school and the new came to a head at the Surat Congress of 1906. It resulted in an open split between the two groups, one of which (the 'extremists') was virtually thrown out of the Congress.

The main cause that gave rise to this split, however, did not remain for long. For, the First World War which shook the entire colonial world and gave rise to the development of national liberation struggles in several countries of Asia could not long keep even the moderates where they were at the time of the Surat Congress. The slogan of self-determination of all peoples which was raised by the statesmen of the Allied Powers, as well as the anti-imperialist sentiments that swept the colonial and dependent peoples throughout the world during the world war, gave even to the most 'loyal,' most 'moderate' politicians of our bourgeoisie, the confidence that they could strengthen themselves politically if only they adopted the technique which the 'extremists' had adopted a decade ago.

This change in the situation paved the way for a rapprochement between the two schools which was solemnized at the famous Lucknow Congress (1916), held within a decade of the Surat split.

This rapprochement between the 'moderates' and 'extremists,' together with a simultaneous agreement between the Indian National Congress and the Muslim League (the well known Lucknow pact providing certain guarantees for the Muslims in the new political set-up, envisaged by the Congress) gave a powerful fillip to the countrywide movement that was slowly developing for 'Home Rule.' The formation of two Home Rule Leagues, one under the leadership of Mrs Beasant and the other led by Tilak, transformed the two agreements of Lucknow into a powerful nationwide mass movement for radical changes in the administrative system of the country.

It was when the entire bourgeoisie was thus entering the arena of national political struggle, when the united bourgeoisie was trying to rally the entire nation around the simple slogan of Home Rule, that Gandhi returned to India with the experience of the unique movement which he had organized and led in South Africa. That was a movement which, like everything else associated with Gandhi, had evoked both admiration as well as ridicule.

Whether belonging to the 'moderate' or 'extremist' school, whether owing loyalty to the Congress or to the League, whether organized under this or that Home Rule League, all politicians of the bourgeoisie admired the manner in which Gandhi had rallied the indentured Indian labour of South Africa and forced its rulers to make partial concessions of their demands. They, however, did not take kindly, either to the philosophical outlook which guided him in his activities, or to the various forms of action and struggle which he resorted to.

All schools of the bourgeois-democratic political movement in the country based themselves on the political movement of the modern bourgeoisie, whose philosophical outlook guided them in their activities. For them, politics of either the 'moderate' or the 'extremist' variety were the application of similar politics (Tory or Liberal) of modern capitalist countries, particularly of Britain. Here, however, was a man who based himself, not on the philosophy, economics, sociology and political science of the modern bourgeoisie, but on Hinduism with a perceptible influence of Christianity. He appeared to them as the very negation of the basic principle of secular politics.

Yet, in the matter of two or three years, they came to accept him as the leader to the most powerful mass movement for the attainment of that very objective for which they had brought about a rapprochement between the 'moderates' and the 'extremists,' and between the Congress and the Muslim League. This will appear to be surprising if we fail to properly appraise the main ingredients of what has come to be known as the 'Gandhian technique,' how this technique was applied to the national-political situation of the post-First World War period, and how it served the cause around which the entire bourgeoisie came to be united at Lucknow in 1916.

The one point of departure between Gandhi, on the one hand, and all other politicians of those days, on the other, was that, unlike the latter, *Gandhi associated himself with the masses of the people, their lives, problems, sentiments and aspirations.* Politics for him was not a matter of high level debate among erudite politicians; it was a matter of selfless service in defence of people's interests and identifying oneself with everything that is of the people. This characteristic feature of Gandhism in action was already visible in the South African struggle in which, as we have noticed, Gandhi drew inspiration and sustenance from the simple and devoted action of the common people.

It was this passion for close association with the common people, this desire to familiarize himself with the living conditions and problems of the people, that enabled Gandhi slowly to evolve a technique of political work which was as different from the 'extremist' school as that of the 'moderate.' The manner in which this technique was used for the first time in India is stated by Tendulkar:

> In the middle of January, Gandhi went to Rajkot and Porbundar to meet his relatives. He always travelled third,

> dressed like a poor passenger. He discarded his cumbrous cloak and white scarf and wore a shirt, a dhoti, and put on a cheap Kashmiri cap.
>
> At Wadhwan, an intermediate station, Motilal, a noted public worker and a tailor by profession, met Gandhi, and acquainted him with the hardships the railway passengers had to undergo, as a result of the notorious Viramgam customs.
>
> 'Are you prepared to go to jail?' Gandhi asked abruptly. 'We will certainly go to jail, provided you lead us,' replied Motilal (I, p. 196).

Gandhi immediately took up the question of the Viramgam customs and began correspondence with the Bombay Government. Though this correspondence yielded no result, the question was settled some time later, when he had occasion to meet the Viceroy: the Viramgam customs cordon was ultimately removed.

This was soon followed up by another case in which, too, the same technique was used—the case of the indigo planters of Champaran in Bihar. Champaran was a mass movement of a far higher order than Viramgam. For, the Champaran issue was not settled without a struggle. It was, in fact, the first mass struggle which Gandhi led in India.

The Champaran struggle is of great importance, firstly, because it was directed against the European planters; secondly, because it rallied, under the banner of struggle for people's demands, some of the finest young intellectuals of the time—those who subsequently became close associates and loyal disciples of Gandhi, such as Rajendra Prasad, Mazarul Haq, J.B. Kripalani, etc.; thirdly, because, despite stiff opposition by the European planters and their protectors in the bureaucracy, Gandhi and his comrades were able to bring the struggle to a successful conclusion. This, therefore, may be said to be the first dress-rehearsal of a type of national struggle which Gandhi was subsequently to lead on more than one occasion. *Here was a movement in which a band of selfless individuals from the middle and upper classes identified themselves with and roused the common people against the powers-that-be in order to secure some well-defined demands.*

Equally important, though in an altogether different respect, was the manner in which Gandhi intervened in the Ahmedabad textile workers' strike of February-March, 1918. This was the first occasion on which Gandhi used his technique in the conflict between workers and capitalists. The way in which he led this struggle and gradually evolved what is commonly known as 'Gandhian trade unionism' is of great importance in the evolution of our national movement, in the evolution of bourgeois leadership over the working-class movement.

> To lead the strike successfully, *Gandhi evolved a new method and laid down these conditions: never to resort to violence; never to molest blacklegs; never to depend on alms;* and to earn bread, during the strike by any other honest labour . . . they (the strikers) attended the meetings in their thousands, and *he reminded them of their pledge and of the duty to maintain peace and self-respect the workers daily paraded the streets of Ahmedabad in peaceful processions, carrying their banner bearing the inscription 'Ek Tek,' 'keep the pledge.'*
>
> The situation began to grow critical. *Gandhi would not allow the weavers to degrade themselves by seeking maintenance out of charity.* But to provide work for thousands of people was not easy. For the first two weeks the workers showed courage and self-restraint and daily held big meetings. *But at last they began to show signs of flagging. Gandhi was afraid of an outbreak of rowdyism on their part, thus losing their cause.* The attendance at the daily meetings also began to dwindle, and despondency and despair were writ large on the faces of those who did attend.
>
> During the strike Gandhi consulted the mill-owners from time to time and entreated them to do justice by the labourers. 'We have our pledge too,' they said. 'Our relations with the labourers are those of parents and children. How

> can we brook the interference of a third party? Where is the room for arbitration?'
>
> 'Twenty days,' in Gandhi's words, 'passed by; *hunger and the mill-owners' emissaries were producing their effect and Satan was whispering to the men that there was no such thing as God on earth who would help them and that vows were dodges resorted to by weaklings.'* The burden of the weavers' grumble was: *It is all right for Gandhi Saheb to tell us to fight unto death. But we have to starve.'*
>
> *On the morning of March 12, it was at a workers' meeting, while Gandhi was still groping, an idea occurred to him. 'Let us both starve,' he said, 'in trying to keep your vows.' Spontaneously these words came to his lips: 'Unless the strikers rally and continue the strike till a settlement is reached or till they leave the mills altogether, I will not touch any food.'*
>
> The strikers were not prepared for these words. They said: 'Not you, but we shall fast. It would be monstrous if you were to fast. Please forgive us for our lapse, we will now remain faithful to our pledge to the end (I, p. 269–70. Emphasis added).

This was, of course, not the first time that Gandhi resorted to a fast. This, however, was the first time that he resorted to it in order to check the militancy of the fighting people. It has added significance in that he was using it, not in relation to a movement in which all classes were participants, but in a working-class struggle. His success in this experiment was an invaluable lesson for the class of which he was the representative, the bourgeoisie. It showed them that here was a technique of struggle which could at once rally the masses and keep them away from militant actions.

Viramgam, Champaran and Ahmedabad, however, were but dress-rehearsals for something still bigger. For, everyone of them was concerned with one or more partial demands of particular sections of the people. There was, on the other hand, the basic demand of the entire people, around which 'moderates' as well as 'extremists,' the Congress as well as the Muslim League, had united at Lucknow—the demand for Home Rule. It was necessary for Gandhi to use his technique to secure this national demand as well.

He did this by developing a movement among the people of the Kheda district of Gujarat around the slogan of '20 recruits from every village.' Those were days, it should be recalled, when the British were in dire need of thousands of Indian recruits for the successful prosecution of the war. The Viceroy had convened a war conference in Delhi to which Gandhi, among others, had been invited. Gandhi spoke in support of the resolution on recruiting, the only condition being that he should be permitted to speak in Hindustani, a condition to which the Viceroy readily agreed.

The manner in which Gandhi conducted himself on this question of recruitment was typical of the clever politician of the bourgeoisie that he was, a politician who, though speaking in terms of such moral values as 'non-violence,' had no qualms of conscience in recruiting young Indians as cannon-fodder for imperialism's war in return for Home Rule. See, for example, how he defended the recruitment campaign as part of the campaign for Swaraj:

> The easiest and straightest way to win Swaraj is to participate in the defence of the Empire. If the Empire perishes, with it will perish our cherished aspirations. Some say that, if we do not win our rights just now, we would be cheated afterwards. The power acquired in defending the Empire will be the power that can secure those rights (I, p. 280).

The hopes entertained by Gandhi and other politicians, however, were not fulfilled. Far from granting the demand for Home Rule, the British launched new attacks on the national movement. The Montagu-Chelmsford proposals for constitutional reform negated all that the national movement had stood for and demanded. Even the most 'moderate' of politicians were dissatisfied with them. Added to them were the Rowlatt Bills arming the government with power to crush all resistance to foreign rule. Public opinion, therefore, was gathering force against the Montagu-Chelmsford proposals and against the Rowlatt Bills.

It was to meet this situation that Gandhi had to use his technique of mass political action within the framework of non-violence. He knew that, though his ideas were being increasingly accepted by broader sections of the people, he would have to meet serious opposition from several respected leaders of the Congress. He, therefore, organized his forces apart from, and independently of, the Congress.

As soon as the notorious Rowlatt Bills were published in the Gazette, Gandhi organized a conference at his Satyagraha Ashram at which a satyagraha pledge was drafted and signed by Vallabhbhai Patel, Sarojini Naidu, B.G. Horniman, Umar Sobani, Shankerlal Banker and Anasuya Behn. The signatories 'solemnly affirmed' that ' . . . in the event of these Bills becoming law and until they are withdrawn we shall refuse civilly to obey these laws and such other laws as a committee to be hereafter appointed, may think fit. . . . ' They further affirmed that 'in this struggle we will faithfully follow truth and refrain from violence to life, person or property.'

Gandhi also started a Satyagraha Sabha in Bombay which began collecting signatures to the satyagraha pledge; as many as 1,200 persons enlisted in the Sabha within a fortnight. A statement issued by the Sabha on March 1919, said: 'The committee contemplated by the satyagraha pledge has advised that for the time being laws regarding prohibitory literature and registration of newspapers may be civilly disobeyed.' The committee selected a list of prohibited literature for dissemination which included *Hind Swaraj*, *Sarvodaya* and *Story of a Satyagrahi*.

In pursuance of the programme of resistance to the Rowlatt Bills, Gandhi proposed a general hartal.

> Satyagraha is a process of self-purification, and ours is a sacred fight and it seems to me to be in the fitness of things that it should be commenced with an act of self-purification. Let all the people of India, therefore, suspend their business

> on that day and observe the day as one for fasting and prayer. The Mussalmans may not fast for more than one day; so the duration of the fast should be twenty-four hours. It is very difficult to say whether all the provinces would respond to this appeal of ours or not, but I feel fairly sure of Bombay, Madras, Bihar and Sind. I think we should have every reason to feel satisfied even if all these places observe hartal fittingly (I, p. 297).

The hartal was fixed for 6 April 1919. It became the beginning of a nationwide movement against the Rowlatt Bills, a movement which spread from one end of the country to the other. It was at Amritsar that it reached the greatest heights of popular enthusiasm and bureaucratic brutality. It was there that, under the brutal regime of the notorious Sir Michael O'Dwyer, assisted by General Dyer, the 6th April demonstration was followed by a series of incidents which culminated in the notorious massacre of Jallianwala Bagh.

The development of the Khilafat agitation brought new strength to Gandhi and his programme of non-cooperation. For this added to the ranks of the champions of non-cooperation almost the entire world of Muslim divines who looked upon the Khilafat question as a question of religion and politics combined. Gandhi at once shrewdly added this to his list of grievances against the British.

In his statement dated 10 March 1920, he said:

> The Khilafat has now become a question of questions. . . . Now a word as to what may be done if the demands are not granted. The barbarous method is warfare, open or secret. This must be ruled out, if only because it is impracticable. If I could but persuade everyone that it is always bad, we should gain all lawful ends much quicker. The power that an individual or a nation forswearing violence can generate is a power that is irresistible (I, p. 345).

Gandhi, however, knew that it was not so much a faith in non-violence but an anxiety to develop a mighty mass revolt that motivated the Muslim divines. He, therefore, did not insist on their adopting his principle of non-violence.

> But Muslims have special Koranic obligations in which Hindus may or may not join. They, therefore, reserve to themselves the right, in the event of the failure of non-cooperation cum nonviolence, in order to enforce justice, to resort to all such methods as may be enjoined by the Islamic scriptures (I, p. 346).

It was a combination of all these circumstances—his own independent organization of a band of satyagrahis around himself; his successful agitation on the living political issues which were uppermost in the minds of the people, such as the Rowlatt Bills and the Punjab wrongs; his alliance with the Muslim divines on the issue of Khilafat—that enabled Gandhi to give, on his own, on 1 August 1920, the signal for the non-cooperation campaign. To the objection raised by leaders like Pandit Malaviya that Gandhi should have awaited the Congress decision, his reply was as follows:

> My loyalty to the Congress requires me to carry out its policy when it is not contrary to my conscience. If I am in a minority, I may not pursue my policy in the name of the Congress. The decision of the Congress on any given question, therefore, does not mean that it prevents a Congressman from any action to the contrary, but if he acts he does so at his own risk and with the knowledge that the Congress is not with him.
>
> Every Congressman, every public body, has the right, it is sometimes their duty to express their own opinion, act upon it even and thus anticipate the verdict of the Congress. Indeed it is the best way of serving the nation (II, p. 3).

Gandhi, together with Maulana Shaukat Ali and others, toured extensively and roused the people on the issues of the

Rowlatt Bills, the Punjab tragedy and Khilafat. This had its effect on the special session of the Congress held in Calcutta from 4–9 September 1920. The Congress, on Gandhi's initiative, adopted its resolution on progressive non-violent non-cooperation. Its operative part states:

> This Congress is further of opinion that there is no course left open for the people of India but to approve of and adopt the policy of progressive non-violent non-cooperation, until the said wrongs are righted and Swaraj is established.
>
> And inasmuch as a beginning should be made by the classes who have hitherto moulded and represented public opinion; and inasmuch as government consolidates its powers through titles and honours bestowed on the people, through schools controlled by it, through its law courts and its legislative councils, and inasmuch as it is desirable, in the present state of the movement, to take the minimum risk and to call for the least sacrifice compatible with the attainment of the desired object, this Congress earnestly advises:
>
> a. Surrender of titles and honorary offices and resignation of nominated posts in local bodies;
>
> b. Refusal to attend government levees, durbars and other official and semi-official functions held by government officials, or in their honour;
>
> c. Gradual withdrawal of children from schools and colleges in the various provinces;
>
> d. Gradual boycott of British courts by lawyers and litigants and establishments of private arbitration courts by them for the settlement of private disputes;
>
> e. Refusal on the part of the military, clerical and labouring classes to offer themselves as recruits for service in Mesopotamia;
>
> f. Withdrawal by the candidates from election to the reformed councils and refusal on the part of the voters to

vote for any candidate who may, despite the Congress advice, offer himself for election;

g. Boycott of foreign goods (II, p. 12–3).

A study of the resolution will show the essential class political character of the programme which Gandhi was initiating. It was candidly stated that non-cooperation was a campaign, in which a beginning should be made by 'the classes who have hitherto moulded and represented public opinion,' i.e., the bourgeoisie and the petty bourgeoisie. Furthermore, the items included in the programme are such that, while they may well irritate and harass the bureaucracy, while they may even create a lot embarrassment and inconvenience to them, do not, even to the slightest extent, shake the essential basis of imperialist rule. It will be noticed that the resolution does not suggest such forms of militant mass action as the industrial workers' general strike or peasants' struggles like non-payment of rent and seizure of land—forms of struggle which touch upon the profits of Indian capitalists and landlords as much as the economic and political basis of the foreign rulers. Even the 'refusal on the part of the military, clerical and labouring classes to offer themselves as recruits' is confined to 'service in Mesopotamia.' It is thus clear that non-violent non-cooperation was conceived not as a form of action which would strike at the roots of the imperialist state structure, but as one which would only put so much pressure on the rulers as would force them to come to terms with the Congress.

It would be useful, in this connection, to recall what Gandhi said on 18 April 1919, on the question of industrial workers' united strike as a form of political action.

> In the course of the satyagraha struggle in South Africa, several thousands of indentured Indians had struck work. *This was a satyagraha strike*, and therefore, entirely peaceful and voluntary. Whilst the strike was going on, the strike of European miners, railway employees, etc., was declared.

> *Overtures were made to me to make common cause with the European strikers. As a satyagrahi, I did not require a moment's consideration to decline to do so. I went further, and for fear of our strike being classed with the strike of Europeans in which methods of violence and use of arms found a prominent place, ours was suspended, and satyagraha from that moment came to be recognized by the Europeans of South Africa as an honourable and honest movement*, in the words of General Smuts, 'a constitutional movement.' *I can do no less at the present critical moment.* I would be untrue to satyagraha if I allowed it by any action of mine to be used as an occasion for feeding violence . . . . (I, p. 317. Emphasis added).

This much-talked-of abhorrence of violence, however, is nothing but the bourgeoisie's natural fear that, once the working class enters the field of political action with its own weapon of struggle—the weapon of political general strike—the movement will go beyond the limits set by it. That is why Gandhi, who had no hesitation to call for 'twenty recruits from every village' to be offered as cannon-fodder in imperialism's bloody wars, shuddered at the few incidents of violence which broke out when the common people, the workers and peasants, entered the field of action as an organized political force.

That again is why he consistently refused to include in his programme, such demands of the middle peasants, poor peasants and the landless poor, as cancellation of usurious debts, drastic reduction of rent, and distribution of landlords' lands among the peasants, etc. The furthest he was prepared to go, and did go, was what was incorporated in the resolution of the Nagpur session of the Congress in December 1921:

> . . . This Congress, while reaffirming the resolution on non-violent non-cooperation, declares that the entire or any party of the non-violent non-cooperation scheme, with the renunciation of voluntary association with the government at one end, and the refusal to pay taxes at the other, should

> be put in force at a time to be determined by either the Indian National Congress or the All India Congress Committee (II, pp. 35–6).

Refusal to pay taxes to the government was thus the utmost limit to which Gandhi was prepared to go —the limit to which the rich peasants and even landlords were prepared to go with him.

Those, however, were days in which the common people refused to be thus restricted in their activities. The very fact that a call for revolt had come—non-violent though its character was to be—made the peasants, the artisans, the workers, etc., rise spontaneously against oppression. The strikes of the industrial and plantation workers and the acute discontent which began to manifest itself among the peasants, led to several incidents which Gandhi had hoped to prevent. Tendulkar describes them as follows:

> Many of the new recruits who worked for the Congress programme lived in a kind of intoxication. The feeling of fear, oppression and frustration completely disappeared. Even in the remote villages, the people talked of the Congress and Swaraj, and what had happened in the Punjab and the Khilafat. The 'Khilafat' bore a very strange meaning in most of the rural areas. People thought it came from *khilaf*—an Urdu word meaning 'against,' and so they took it to mean 'opposed to government.' There was a strange mixture of nationalism, religion and mysticism (II, p. 46).

Gandhi's reaction was characteristic of the man and the movement which he was to lead for nearly three decades. Far from being inspired by the tremendous response of the masses to his call for non-cooperation with the 'Satanic government,' he was alarmed at the lack of what he called 'that non-violent and truthful atmosphere which alone can justify mass civil disobedience.'

He was alarmed at first during the Rowlatt Act agitation when 'I retraced my steps, called it a Himalayan miscalculation, humbled myself before God and man, and stopped not merely mass civil disobedience but even my own, which I knew was intended to be civil and non-violent.'

It was, however, not till the Chauri Chaura incident of 1922, (which he called his 'bitterest humiliation') that he came to realize that the mass civil disobedience which he had visualized, and for which he was preparing, could often go completely beyond his control. He then decided to suspend the civil disobedience movement.

Chauri Chaura was not an isolated incident. It had been preceded by the Malabar rebellion, commonly known as the Moplah rebellion, in which Gandhi's call for non-cooperation with the British had been integrated with the anti-landlord demands of the peasantry and which, therefore, drew into its fold tens of thousands of the oppressed peasantry of Malabar. In several other parts of the country too, hundreds of youths and elderly men responded to Gandhi's call to boycott schools, colleges and courts and to become whole time messengers of the spirit of non-cooperation. They went among the peasantry and started voicing their demands for rent reduction, relief from exorbitant taxation, etc. As a matter of fact, the very movement which, according to Gandhi, should be begun by 'the classes who have hitherto moulded and represented public opinion' was going beyond the limits set by those classes and becoming a real national movement.

Further, once they were drawn into the movement, this new class, the peasantry, threw up its own forms of struggle and its own forms of organization. This was clearly visible in the Malabar rebellion in which, such typically peasant forms of revolutionary action were resorted to as the burning of landlords' records, the destruction of registry offices, attacks on government offices, disarming of the police, setting up of people's courts, and distribution of food-grains and other things in the landlords' mansions.

Chauri Chaura also showed that, once the peasantry comes face to face with the organs of state power, it, inevitably, is led to forms of action outside the definition of non-violence laid down by Gandhi.

Hence Gandhi's confession: 'Madras (Malabar) did give the warning, but I heeded it not. But God spoke clearly through Chauri Chaura.' He had no doubt that the police in Chauri Chaura 'had given much provocation.' It was this provocation of the police that made 'the mob' set fire to the *thana* and kill policemen. But Gandhi was not prepared to condone this 'mob violence,' even if it were the result of police provocation. It was clear to him that, once the peasants were aroused and brought into action, such clashes between them and the organs of British rule were certain to repeat themselves. This was so terrible a prospect for him to even contemplate that he decided that the very continuation of the movement would mean 'the denial of our oath and sin against God.' Hence the decision to suspend civil disobedience.

First Breach

A large number of Gandhi's lieutenants and colleagues did not see why he should be so perturbed at certain incidents that had taken place in the course of the non-cooperation movement. Their reaction to Gandhi's decision to suspend the movement is described by Tendulkar:

> The sudden stoppage of the movement came as a shock. The Bardoli decision created consternation among the Congress leaders, most of whom were in prison, and left the rank and file angry. Gandhi was attacked from all sides. Motilal Nehru, Lajpat Rai and others sent from prison angry letters to Gandhi protesting against his position. Why, asked Motilal Nehru, should a town at the foot of the Himalayas be penalized, if a village at Cape Comorin failed to observe non-violence? Isolate Chauri Chaura and Gorakhpur, go on with civil disobedience, individual and mass (II, p. 117).

This was the first breach in the unity that Gandhi had been able to forge in the ranks of the Congress since the days of the anti-Rowlatt Bill and Khilafat agitation. Non-violent non-cooperation was the programme through which he had been able to rally the moderates as well as the extremists: his insistence on non-violence satisfied the moderates, while his call for anti-imperialist mass action roused the extremists. However, the horror with which Gandhi looked upon the militant actions of the masses, the haste in which he decided to suspend civil disobedience, brought to the forefront all those basic questions around which the Congress ranks had earlier been divided.

What was to be the path of struggle for the realization of the national demand? Was it to be peaceful negotiations with the British, or militant struggle against them? Was it to be a path of rallying the mass of our people in determined actions against the regime or a path of reliance on the constitutional machinery to secure more and more reforms? These questions which had once divided the moderates from the extremists once again came to the forefront, but in another form.

Motilal Nehru, Lajpat Rai and others who protested against Gandhi's action in suspending the civil disobedience movement were by no means militant anti-imperialists. Some of them (like Motilal Nehru) had actually been in the camp of the moderates even in the earlier period. They had come to accept the leadership of Gandhi because they realized that his method of rallying the masses against British imperialism would put a good deal of pressure on imperialism. They hoped that this pressure would force imperialism to negotiate with the Congress and that, by skilful utilization of mass actions unleashed under Gandhi's leadership, they could secure more and more constitutional reforms. They were, therefore, not worried over some 'mob violence' here or there; these would undoubtedly take place for which the Congress would and should abjure all responsibility. They did not share Gandhi's pessimism that this would take the movement beyond the limits considered safe by their own class. Hence their anger when they heard of Gandhi's decision.

But now that the suspension of the civil disobedience had become an accomplished fact, they raised the inevitable question: what next? They had no patience with those who argued that the masses would slowly imbibe the ideas of non-violence, thus making it possible for the Congress to make adequate preparations for the launching of that type of non-violent struggle which was visualized by Gandhi. Looking upon Gandhi's technique of non-violent non-cooperation from the purely practical point of view of successfully forcing the British to negotiate with the Congress, they came to the conclusion that, if the suspension of the civil disobedience movement was to be endorsed, then the Congress should look for new tactics.

It was in this search for new tactics that they came to the conclusion that the newly-formed legislative councils should be used, rather than boycotted. They argued that, while boycott of legislatures was correct so long as it was an inseparable part of the programme of non-violent non-cooperation leading to countrywide civil disobedience, it had no meaning at a time when civil disobedience was not thought of. Not only did they openly express these views, but they went to the extent of forming a new party pledged to carry out this programme—the Swaraj Party. This was, of course, confined to a minority of Congressmen: the Gaya session of the Congress held in 1922 rejected the programme of council entry by 1740 votes against 890.

This was an indication of the dominant militant mood of the mass of Congressmen. However, though a minority, the Swarajists were enormously influential inside the Congress; firstly, because they were headed by some of the most well-known top leaders of the Congress; and secondly, because the opponents of council entry had no alternate programme of action.

The struggle between the Swarajists and the 'no-changers' had started and developed while Gandhi was in jail. (Ironically enough, a few days after the suspension of the civil disobedience movement, Gandhi was arrested and put in jail.) By the time of his release, therefore, the Congress had already been divided into two camps—it was almost on the point of being split into two organizations. Gandhi, therefore, applied himself to the problem of healing the breach and uniting the two wings of the Congress. He sensed the atmosphere and found that council entry had become a settled fact. He knew that a question on which such sharp differences existed in the leadership of the Congress could not be settled by a majority vote. He posed the question thus:

> The question is, what is to be done regarding the council entry as a settled fact? Are the non-cooperators to keep up their hostility against the Swarajist methods, or are they to remain neutral and even help wherever it is possible or consistent with their principles? . . . If the work of the Swarajists prospers and the country benefits, such an ocular

> demonstration cannot but convince honest sceptics like me of our error, and I know the Swarajists to be patriotic enough to retrace their steps when experience has disillusioned them. I would, therefore, be no party to putting any obstacles in their way or to carrying on any propaganda against the Swarajists' entry into the legislatures, though I cannot actively help them in a project in which I do not believe (II, p. 172).

This was the way in which Gandhi gave his blessings to the Swarajists. It was certainly not in conformity with the desires of his 'no-changer' lieutenants, such as Rajagopalachari, Vallabhbhai Patel, Rajendra Prasad, etc. He had to, therefore, patiently argue with them that the superiority of their 'no-change' tactics was to be proved, not by continuous opposition to the Swarajist programme, but by continuous and systematic work outside the legislature. After all, he told them, the Swarajist's preoccupation with council work was not going to yield much success in the struggle for freedom; success could be achieved only through hard work among the masses, work towards preparing the country for the struggle that was undoubtedly ahead. He advised them to concentrate on organizing the people, the only basis on which the national cause could advance.

It was through such skilful yet persuasive arguments that Gandhi was able, in the end, to persuade the Congress, not only to recognize the Swarajist Party as an integral part of the Congress, but to make it the centre of its political activity. At the same time, he made it obligatory for the Swarajists to engage themselves in such activities as the promotion of khadi, eradication of untouchability, propagation of Hindi, etc.

> And I have come to the conclusion that it is in the interest of the country to give the Swaraj Party the fullest possible chance of working out its own programme without let or hindrance from no-changers. The latter are not bound to participate

> in its activity if they do not like it. They are free and bound, as the Swarajists are bound, to pursue the constructive programme only. They are free also to retain their individual non-cooperation. But suspension by the Congress means that non-cooperators can derive no support or strength from the Congress. They must derive all their strength from within. And that is their test and trial (II, p. 22).

The next few years, therefore, were years in which Gandhi and his no-changer followers concentrated on the advancement of the constructive programme. It was in pursuance of this programme that Gandhi organized the All India Khadi Board. It was to popularize this programme that he toured extensively throughout the country. Wherever he went, he popularized the programme of *Khadi*, argued against the untouchability, and championed the programme of a *lingua franca*, etc.

The manner in which he went about from place to place, popularizing the cause of the constructive programme, has several features which enabled him to mobilize the masses, but prevent them from taking militant anti-imperialist political action.

The most notable feature among these is that rarely did Gandhi refer to political questions. Take his speeches of 1921–22 where he often referred to the Punjab atrocities, the Rowlatt Bills and the Khilafat movement—all directed against the British government. Contrast them with his speeches of 1924–28, when almost all the speeches were concerned with social and spiritual questions. He was rousing the people, not against the political and economic system under which they were living, but against certain social evils and for certain spiritual values.

Secondly, though he did not rouse the people against imperialism, landlordism and other forms of oppression and exploitation; he spoke of the miseries of the people, the inequality that existed in the country, the necessity of redressing the grievances of the people. There was not one section of the people whose problems he did not study, whose miserable conditions he did not bring out, for whose comfort and solace he did not plead with his audience. It was this that enabled him to attract the various sections of the poor and downtrodden masses.

Look, for example, how he talked with the *devadasis*. 'Supposing,' he asked them, 'I took you away and gave you sufficient food, clothing, education and clean surroundings, would you leave this life of shame and come with me?' The reply was 'Yes.' He referred to it in his speech, and poured out his heart:

> As I was talking to them and understanding the hidden meaning of the thing, my whole soul rose in rebellion against the custom of taking minor girls for immoral purposes. Calling them *devadasis*, we insult God Himself in the name of religion. . . . (II, p. 371).

Look again how he replies to the taxpayers of Bangalore who wanted to hear him on municipal problems:

> I am glad that you have introduced here compulsory primary education. I congratulate you on your spacious roads, your splendid lighting and your beautiful parks. But while I can infer from your address that the middle and the upper classes must be happy here, I wonder if you have a poor class at all and, if you have, what you are doing to keep them clean and healthy. Have you shared in their hardships and their sorrows? Have you ever thought of the conditions in which the sweepers and the scavengers live? Have you ensured a cheap milk supply for the infants, the aged and the infirm of the poorer classes? Are you sure that the foodstuffs that your provision dealers sell are clean and unadulterated? . . . I can ask you many more questions. If you have a satisfactory reply to each of them, I can congratulate you. But if you have none, then I beseech you to give them your most earnest consideration (II, pp. 363–64).

Thirdly, though speaking in the name of, and in a language understandable to, the masses of the toiling people, Gandhi was firmly opposed to anything that would rally the masses against the existing social system. His reply to Saklatwala, who visited India in 1927 and had a long interview with him, is characteristic. He concedes that 'Comrade Saklatwala is dreadfully in earnest. His sincerity is transparent. His passion for the poor is unquestioned.' But, says Gandhi, 'Comrade Saklatwala disdains to study facts,' 'ignores India and Indian conditions.'

And what are these 'facts' and 'conditions' which Comrade Saklatwala ignored?

> I do not regard capital to be the enemy of labour. I hold their coordination to be perfectly possible. The organization of labour that I undertook in South Africa, Champaran or Ahmedabad was in no spirit of hostility to the capitalists. The resistance in each case, and to the extent it was thought necessary, was wholly successful. My ideal is equal distribution but, so far as I can see, it is not to be realized. I, therefore, work for equitable distribution. This I seek to attain through khaddar. And since its attainment must sterilize British exploitation at its centre, it is calculated to purify the British connection. Hence, in this sense, khaddar leads to Swaraj (II, p. 340).

In other words, the khadi programme was a programme of organizing labour-capital coordination and the 'purification' of the British connection.

Fourthly, the constructive programme was a programme of action—action in the sense that everybody who swore by it had to *do* something. It was one of the greatnesses of Gandhi that he mastered the art of giving some job to everybody who went to him. You may be a worker or a peasant or a professional; whatever you may be, Gandhi had something which kept you busy. And in thus keeping you busy, he gave you the exhilarating idea that you were serving the great cause of the spiritual, economic and political regeneration of your country. It was this that he accomplished through his message of charkha, the message of other cottage industries, the message of Hindi, the message of the uplift of the untouchables, the message of social reform in general.

Gandhi roused you to activity on all these issues and created in you the sense of doing all these things as the necessary preparation for the struggle for Swaraj. Behind all the separate items of the constructive programme was the message of resistance to imperialism. It was through this that Gandhi could create hundreds of determined cadres for the national movement under his leadership, who were fired with the spirit of service and sacrifice, but were the least 'tainted''with the 'sin' of that revolutionary fervour which may endanger the very existence of the class which Gandhi represented.

Fifthly, the most remarkable feature of Gandhi's activities in those years was the skilful way in which he integrated the ostensibly non-political constructive programme with the avowedly political activities of the Swarajists. While allowing the Swarajists to have the satisfaction that it was they who were carrying on 'real' political work, i.e., the work of exposing and fighting the government with all the available means and weapons of struggle; while equally allowing the constructive workers to have the satisfaction that it was they who were preparing the country for the inevitable future struggle against imperialism; Gandhi was able to hold the reins of both the Swarajist and constructive wings of the Congress and thus unify the leadership and ranks of the Congress under him.

Blessing the Swarajists, he laid down the line which they should pursue inside the legislatures—the line of 'endeavouring to give strength to the constructive programme of the Congress.' He asked them not to follow

> a general policy of obstruction . . . but to move resolutions requiring the central and provincial governments, as the case may be, first, to make all their cloth purchases in hand-woven and hand-spun khaddar; secondly, to impose a prohibitive duty on foreign cloth; . . . If the government refuses to enforce such a resolution when carried in the legislature, I should notify them to dissolve them and take the vote of the electors

> on the specific points. If the government would not dissolve, I should resign my seat and prepare the country for civil disobedience (II, pp. 172–73).

While claiming that he himself was a constructive worker rather than a Swarajist, he took keen interest in all the activities of the Swarajists. He gave his blessings to the well-known tactics adopted by the Swarajists and their allies in the central legislature—the moving of the famous resolution on national demand and the pursuing of the tactics of obstruction and walkout when it was not accepted. He gave the enormous weight and authority of his name in favour of whatever efforts were made by the Swarajists to open negotiations with the British rulers, but kept himself in the background till these negotiations reached a stage in which he felt that there was a certain amount of possibility of success.

It is remarkable, in this connection, how he expressed himself on the negotiations between Deshbandhu Das, the Swarajist leader, and Lord Birkenhead, the secretary of state for India. In the course of a speech in Calcutta on 1 May 1925 he said that, instead of entering into diplomatic relations with 'matchless diplomats' from England he preferred to concentrate on the constructive programme for developing the power of India from within. However, a few days later, on 20th June, he himself made a public appeal to Englishmen to respond to the offer made by the Deshbandhu:

> The Faridpur speech had a great purpose behind it. It was a generous response to the Anglo-Indian friends who were anxious for the great patriot to make his position clear and make the first approach. He made it. The cruel hand of death has removed the author of the gesture from our midst. But I would like to assure Englishmen who may be still doubtful about the sincerity of Deshbandhu's motive that, throughout my stay in Darjeeling, the one thing that stuck me most was his utter sincerity about that utterance. Cannot this glorious

death be utilized to heal the wounds and forget distrust? (II, p. 255).

In short, the technique that he slowly evolved in the post-non-cooperation days was one of allowing the Swarajists to take advantage of every opportunity to put forward the demand for Swaraj and to open negotiations with the British government while, at the same time, utilizing the energies of tens of thousands of selfless constructive workers to build up a network of organizations and thus preparing the country for another round of non-violent struggle, if the negotiations were to end in failure.

Not only was this eminently suited to the political requirements of the bourgeoisie, but it was a policy which could be successfully carried out by Gandhi, who combined in himself the direct leadership of the constructive programme and the indirect leadership of the Swarajists in the matter of negotiations. It was his ability to meet these requirements of the bourgeoisie that made him the undisputed leader not only of the constructive workers, but also of the Swarajists; not only of Congressmen, but also of liberals and other bourgeois parties and groups.

On Poorna Swaraj

While the Congress under Gandhi's inspiration was carrying out the council entry-cum-constructive programme, two new forces were appearing on the arena of national politics—the forces of communalism (Hindu and Muslim) and the forces of radical anti-imperialism. Both began to emerge on the scene after the suspension of the civil disobedience movement and as a result of the sense of frustration and political confusion that flowed from it. Each, in its own peculiar way, hampered Gandhi and his colleagues in the Swarajist and the constructive worker camps in the carrying out of their respective programmes.

The split which occurred inside the Congress when civil disobedience was suspended, was soon followed by differences within the Swarajist camp itself. The original idea of using the council chambers for purposes of exposure and propaganda was soon given up by a section of the original Swarajists in favour of the so-called policy of 'responsive cooperation,' on the basis of which they formed their own separate group. This difference on the question of concrete tactics to be pursued inside the legislatures quickly gave way to further differences, which assumed a communal character.

Many of the non-cooperators of the 1921 period became champions of the sectional claims of this or that community. Communal organizations in general, and those of Hindus and Muslims in particular, began to grow and make tall claims for their respective communities. What was worse, these sectional claims of particular communities found their champions even among well-known leaders of the Congress, some of whom helped Hindu communal organizations while others helped their Muslim counterparts.

Communalism, however, did not confine itself to the making of claims and counter-claims at the top level alone; it enveloped the whole public life of the country. Issues like cow slaughter, music before mosques, conversion and reconversion of individuals from one religion to another—all these assumed serious proportions and, in several instances, led to clashes and even murders. The atmosphere of communal unity, which had been generated in the days of non-cooperation and Khilafat and which gave a national, democratic character to the movement, gave place to one of acute tension.

Gandhi's reaction to this situation was characteristic. The sensitive soul in him revolted at the internecine quarrel that had destroyed the exhilarating atmosphere of the glorious days of non-cooperation. His heart bled at the inhuman deeds perpetrated by people who spoke in the name of God, but acted as agents of Satan. Against the indescribable horrors that had been perpetrated in the name of religion, he entered his first public protest by undertaking a fast for bringing peace and harmony.

This had, of course, a temporary effect. Leaders of different communities came together and promised Gandhi that they would do their utmost to preserve communal peace. But it had no lasting effect on the public life of the country. On the contrary, the further the Congress under Gandhi's leadership advanced in the direction of successful struggle for Swaraj, the worse became the communal situation. At every subsequent phase in the struggle against imperialism, the communal situation became the biggest stumbling block in Gandhi's way. In the end, it led to a distorted type of Swaraj which was a blow against all that Gandhi stood for—the partition of India into the Hindu-majority Indian Union and Muslim-majority Pakistan—and his own tragic end at the hands of an assassin risen from the ranks of the Hindu communalists.

Gandhi's reaction to the emergence of the force of communalism was, however, not confined to mere humanitarian horror at the atrocities that were committed in the name of religion. Being, above all, a politician striving to unite the various classes, communities and sections of the Indian people in the struggle for Swaraj, he quickly realized that the communal problem should be seen not only as a human problem of relation between people following different religions, but also as a practical, *political* problem. He saw it as a problem of adjusting the claims and counter-claims of different sections of the Indian people in the matter of sharing the power that was sought to be wrested from the British rulers.

Swaraj was impossible to achieve unless there was a certain amount of agreement as to what constituted its form and content, unless different sections of the people were made to understand what they could expect from the new constitutional-political set-up that would be established on its attainment. This was all the more important at a time when, lacking any rational political argument against conceding the demand for Swaraj, the British rulers were utilizing the division and disunity among the various communities as the most important argument in their favour.

Lord Birkenhead, the then secretary of state for India, threw out a challenge to the Indian politicians to draw up a constitution that would be acceptable to all sections of the people. He was confident that the claims and counter-claims that would inevitably be made by the Hindus and Muslims against each other and the Christians, the untouchable castes, etc. against both, not to speak of such 'interests' as Europeans, the princes, the landlords, etc., would completely negate the national and democratic demands that would be put forward by the Congress and other non-communal democratic elements.

This was a challenge that had to be taken up if the Congress, as the premier national political organization of the country, was to survive. And it was taken up. The Congress took initiative in convening an All Parties Committee with the elder Nehru (Motilal) as its chairman and the younger (Jawaharlal) as its secretary. The report that it produced (the Nehru Report) and the draft constitution which it put forward became the rallying point of big sections of politicians of all communities, though vital differences still persisted on such questions as separate electorates, reservation of seats, distribution of powers between the centre and provinces, etc.

While this unity of the Congress, liberals and other sections of the topmost politicians around the Nehru Report was a big achievement of the Swarajist leaders under Gandhi's blessing, a challenge to the whole approach underlying this unity was coming from the second of the two new forces mentioned earlier—the forces of radical anti-imperialism.

The suspension of civil disobedience had roused the indignation of large sections of ordinary Congress workers and volunteers. A feeling of being betrayed by their own leaders, at the very moment when the enemy was at its weakest, had gripped hundreds of thousands of Congressmen. They felt that something was wrong in the way Gandhi led the movement, but were not at one with the new politics that was sought to be imported into the Congress by Das, the elder Nehru, the elder Patel and others. They were, therefore, in the camp of no-changers in the sense that they were against council entry. They, however, had very little in common with the politics of the no-changers, which, for the time being, were, after all, those of the constructive programme. Therefore, dissatisfied with both, they felt helpless and frustrated, sensing that something was wrong and yet unable to locate it, desiring a change yet unable to find what that change ought to be.

It was into the midst of such disillusioned Congressmen that new ideas began to come from abroad—ideas of militant anti-imperialism (from Ireland and Egypt), ideas of radical social and cultural change (from Turkey), ideas of socialism (from Soviet Russia). Together with the entry of these ideas into the minds of disillusioned young Congressmen, new classes and sections of society were making their debut in active public life.

Particularly important in this connection was the rise of the working class as a force to reckon with in the 1920s. The strike movement that had become a feature of the industrial and political life of the country, preceding and during the non-cooperation movement, was slowly consolidating itself into trade unions, the initial form of class organization of the working class. The All India Trade Union Congress, which came on the scene of industrial relations, and which was used by the government as the machinery for selecting delegates for the International Labour Organization (ILO) conferences, was based on a growing number of trade unions. Many of these unions were led by young nationalists who, thorough their very association with the working class, began to slowly imbibe the ideas to which the working class is particularly attached—ideas of radical anti-imperialism and social justice.

Naturally, therefore, the young nationalists who went to the working class and actively participated in their struggles became the core of the movement for the new ideals of radical anti-imperialism, social and cultural revolution and socialism. Scattered groups of socialists and even communists began to emerge in the industrial cities of Bombay and Calcutta. They slowly spread to other centres of political activity and, in the end, led to the formation of such organizations as the Workers' and Peasants' Party.

It was, however, not only the section which went to the working class that became the vehicle for the communication of the new ideas of radical anti-imperialism. Even among those who confined themselves to the urban petty bourgeoisie, these ideas began to grow and crystallize. Some of them were wedded to the cult of individual terrorism. The post-non-cooperation days witnessed a rapid growth of such groups, and a corresponding growth in the number of 'actions' resorted to by them. There were, however, other groups which were not wedded to individual terrorism but who, nevertheless, refused to accept either the philosophy of non-violence and constructive programme preached by Gandhi, or the politics of council entry adopted by the Swarajists. Heroic and self-sacrificing as they were, these radical anti-imperialists drew the admiration of large masses of Congressmen, many of whom did not agree with their politics, yet found in them the true representatives of a nation struggling to be free.

These radical anti-imperialists were, of course, organized in scattered local groups without any organized all-India leadership to guide their activities. There were very sharp and vital differences of policy which separated one groups from another—differences as sharp as, if not sharper than, those between the Swarajists and no-changers, the responsive cooperators and the other Swarajists, the Congressmen and the liberals, etc. Yet, the wide public discussion that followed Lord Birkenhead's challenge to the nation and the Congress response to it by way of the All Parties Conference and the Nehru Report, provided a central issue on which all these groups came to be united—the issue of the nation's goal.

As opposed to the whole camp of politicians, who rallied themselves around the Nehru Report, the radical anti-imperialist youth of the country united itself under the banner of complete independence. The unity that was brought about between Gandhi, Motilal Nehru, the moderates and others was based on their common acceptance of the idea that the goal of India's struggle was Dominion status, as enjoyed by Canada, Australia and other countries of the British Empire. It was to this that the challenge came from the united voice of all those who were organized in the various groups of radical anti-imperialists. They demanded that the Congress should categorically reject the idea of Dominion status and make complete separation of India from the British Empire the objective of her struggle.

This was a demand which rallied not only the radical groups organized outside the Congress, but also drew into its fold big sections of radicals from inside the Congress itself. Nor were they confined to the ranks of ordinary Congressmen; among them could be seen such eminent Congressmen as Jawaharlal Nehru, who was then the general secretary of the Congress and also acted as the general secretary of the All-Parties Committee; Subhas Chandra Bose, on whom had fallen the mantle of Deshbandhu Das as the leader of the Bengal Congress; Srinivasa Iyengar, who was the president of the Gauhati Session of the Congress; Satyamurti, one of the effective parliamentarians of the Congress, etc. The slogan of Poorna Swaraj was so powerful and appealing to the mass of Congressmen that the 1927 session of the Congress (Madras) adopted a resolution, declaring it as the goal of the Congress.

Gandhi was opposed to the whole idea. As he had made himself clear in the days of the First World War, he was a friend of the British Empire. His only quarrel with the Empire was that Indians and other subjects of the Emperor were not allowed to enjoy what he considered to be the benefits of their connection with the Empire. His demand, therefore, was only that Indians should have the same rights as the Canadians, the Australians and the New Zealanders. He totally disapproved of the action of the Madras Congress and made no secret of it:

> The Congress stultifies itself by repeating year after year resolutions of this character when it knows that it is not capable of carrying them into effect. By passing such resolutions, we make an exhibition of our impotance, become the laughing-stock of critics and involve the contempt of our adversary . . . . We have almost sunk to the school-boy's debating society (II, p. 402).

The two years that elapsed between the Madras session of 1927, when the Congress adopted complete independence as its *goal*, and the Lahore Session of 1929, when it adopted it as the *immediate objective*, as opposed to distant goal, were years of furious controversy. Both Mahatma Gandhi as well as Motilal Nehru tried their best to convince Jawaharlal Nehru, Subhas Bose, Srinivasa Iyengar and other leaders of the complete independence school that they were fighting for a word, that there was no difference in substance between Dominion status and complete independence. Gandhi, for example, wrote in *Young India* (12 January 1928):

> I submit that Swaraj is an all-satisfying goal for all time. We the English-educated Indians often unconsciously make the terrible mistake of thinking that the microscopic minority of the English-speaking Indians is the whole of India. I defy any one to give for independence a common Indian word intelligible to the masses. Our goal at any rate may be known by an indigenous word understood by the three hundred millions. And we have such a word in Swaraj, first used in the

> name of the nation by Dadabhai Naoroji. It is infinitely greater than and includes independence (II, p. 428).

Almost a year later, concluding the Calcutta Session of the Congress, Motilal Nehru said:

> I would give you one word of advice. Erase from your mind from today those two terms borrowed from foreign language, namely, independence and Dominion status, and take to the words Swaraj and azadi. Let us, work for Swaraj by whatever name we might call it (II, p. 441).

This open opposition of the two topmost leaders of the Congress, however, did not weaken the movement for replacing the goal of Dominion status with that of complete independence. On the other hand, the more days that passed since the Madras Congress, the greater became the strength of the movement. The Independence of India League, organized by Jawaharlal Nehru, Subhas Bose, Srinivasa Iyengar, Satyamurti and others became the rallying point for thousands of young Congressmen and thus brought about what subsequently may have developed into an alternative leadership for the Congress.

Sensing this situation, Gandhi tried to effect a compromise between the Dominion status and complete independence schools. The compromise was that, while adhering to the goal of complete independence, the Congress would accept Dominion status, provided it was conceded within a year. If, however, this was not conceded within the stipulated period, the Gandhi-Motilal Nehru groups of leaders would themselves agree to have the Congress committed to complete independence and, what is more, organize non-violent non-cooperation for its achievement.

This compromise was put in the form of a resolution to be moved at the Calcutta (1928) Session of the Congress. This was a compromise to which Jawaharlal Nehru and Subhas Bose had, at first, agreed. But, due to pressure from the ranks of their own followers, they had in the end to move an amendment to the compromise resolution. Gandhi, however, could carry a majority of the delegates behind the compromise resolution, but the very fact that as many as 973 delegates voted against waiting for another year (as against 1350 for such waiting) showed how great was the impatience with the politics of Dominion status and negotiations.

The British government, however, was not prepared to oblige the Gandhi-Motilal leadership by conceding their demand. While the majority of Congressmen had come to a position in which they would not be satisfied even with Dominion status, the British were not prepared for anything more than provincial autonomy, and that too with all the possible 'safeguards' that could be provided for such minority 'interests' as the Europeans, landlords, etc., not to speak of the 'safeguards' for the Muslims and other minority communities. The Gandhi-Motilal leadership, in collaboration with the moderates like Sapru, carried on their efforts at negotiations down to the very last moment. Even as late as on the eve of the Lahore Session (1929) of the Congress in which the 'year of grace' given by the Calcutta Congress would expire, a final attempt was made to find some basis of agreement between the Congress and the British government.

It is characteristic of Gandhi that, while thus striving to open negotiations with the British, he was preparing for the second contingency visualized at the Calcutta Congress, e.g., the demand for complete independence. He realized that this contingency could be faced only by making such a gesture to the radical anti-imperialist section inside the Congress as would unite the entire Congress under his own leadership. Such a gesture was made by him when he proposed the name of Jawaharlal Nehru for the presidency of the Lahore Session of the Congress.

There were many among his followers who demanded that, since this was a session which was likely to give a call for countrywide direct action, he himself should stand at the head of the Congress. There were others who proposed the name of the younger (Vallabhbhai) Patel, because they thought that since he was the leader of the successful peasant struggle in Bardoli—which came to be looked upon as a model for any future struggle for the realization of complete independence—it was proper that he should be asked to accept the presidency. Gandhi rejected both these proposals.

Rebutting the arguments of those who feared that 'this transfer of power from the old to the young' might prove disastrous to the Congress, he said:

> A lover of discipline, he (Jawaharlal) has shown himself to be capable of rigidly submitting to it even where it has seemed irksome. He is undoubtedly an extremist thinking far ahead of his surroundings. But he is humble and practical enough not to force the pace to the breaking point (II, pp. 489–90).

Addressing the youth in general, Gandhi told them that they were on trial and asked them to take Jawaharlal's election as a tribute to their services.

Referring to steam 'which becomes a mighty power only when it allows itself to be imprisoned in a strong little reservoir and produces tremendous motion,' he went on to say, 'even so have the youth of the country of their free will to allow their inexhaustible energy to be imprisoned, controlled and set free in strictly measured and required quantities.'

Jawaharlal's election as the President of the Congress was thus a step through which Gandhi brought together the old Swarajists and no-changers. It was also the first step he took in the direction of 'imprisoning, controlling and setting free in strictly measured and required quantities' the anti-imperialist ferment that was then sweeping the country, especially among the youth. He took the initiative in seeing that the left movement—the movement in the direction of modern socialism—was brought within the framework of his own (bourgeois) leadership, rather than allowing it to develop on independent class lines.

The election of Jawaharlal Nehru as president of the Congress and the declaration of complete independence at the Lahore Session were hailed by the champions of complete independence as their victory. Behind this victory, however, can be seen a real compromise between the two schools of Dominion status and complete independence—a compromise which had been attempted at Calcutta but failed. The basis of this compromise can be seen in two important documents from which Tendulkar gives extracts.

In an article written a few weeks before the Lahore Congress, Gandhi said:

> I can wait for the Dominion status constitution, if I can get the real Dominion status in action, if today, there is a real change of heart, a real desire on the part of the British people to see India a free and self-respecting nation and on the part of the officials in India a true spirit of service . . . *My conception of Dominion status implies present ability to sever the British connection if I wish to.* (II, p. 502. emphasis added).

Jawaharlal Nehru in his presidential address at Lahore almost echoed the sentiments of Gandhi:

> Independence for us means complete freedom from British domination and British imperialism. *Having attained our freedom, I have no doubt that India will welcome all attempts at world cooperation and federation, and will even agree to give up part of her own independence to a larger group of which she is an equal member* (II, p. 504. emphasis added).

In other words, while Gandhi accepted complete independence with his own interpretation of it, Jawaharlal agreed to consider some limits to independence after it was won.

This narrowing down of the difference, together with the realization that only a mass struggle would force the British to concede the nation's demand, regardless of whether it was the one conceived by Gandhi or that conceived by Nehru, made it necessary for them to agree to carry out the Calcutta Congress decision on complete independence, and start preparations for a struggle. That is why Gandhi declared at the Lahore Congress: 'We are now entering upon a new era. Our objective and not our distant goal is complete independence.'

Salt Satyagraha Phase

The nation was indeed entering upon a new era. A new upsurge of mass struggle was unfolding itself. Thousands of young men and women who had felt frustrated at the suspension of the 1922 civil disobedience movement came forward to offer themselves as disciplined soldiers in the cause of independence. The call given by the Working Committee to observe 26 January 1930, as the 'Independence Day' evoked glorious mass demonstrations. The inspiring document issued by the Working Committee headed by Jawaharlal Nehru (the Independence Pledge) was not only a powerful indictment of the misdeeds and atrocities of the alien rulers, but a stirring call to the patriotic youth of the country to go forward till the last vestiges of foreign rule were eliminated. Towns and villages vied with each other in celebrating the historic day. In the cities, led by Calcutta and Bombay, scores of thousands met and took the great resolve and in the countryside thousands of villagers assembled at numerous village meetings (III, p. 12).

The decision to break the Salt Laws and the march to Dandi which Gandhi undertook were looked upon by the people as the beginning of a big mass movement for securing complete independence. And when the campaign for mass defiance of the Salt Laws started, first at Dandi by Gandhi himself and later by other leaders in several places all over the country, men, women and children flocked to witness the defiance of the British-made law. Undaunted by arrests, lathi charges and firings, people flocked to the banner of the Congress and participated in the movement.

The mood of the people can be gauged from the following description:

> There was firing in Calcutta, Madras, Karachi and lathi charges all over India. Processions and meetings were

banned. People retaliated by intensive picketing of foreign cloth shops and liquor booths. . . .

On 18 April police armouries at Chittagong were raided. The revolutionary upsurge reached its highest point in Peshawar where huge mass demonstrations were held on 23 April. The next day, Khan Abdul Ghaffar Khan, leader of the newly-formed Khudai Khidmatgar—Servants of God—or the Red Shirts, was arrested. Thousands of people surrounded the place of his detention and there was a mammoth demonstration in Peshawar. Armoured cars were sent to cow down angry demonstrators; one armoured car was burnt, its occupants escaping; thereupon wholesale firing on the crowds was followed by hundreds of deaths and casualties. Two platoons of the Second Battalion of the 18th Royal Garhwali Rifles, Hindu troops in the midst of a Muslim crowd, refused to fire, broke ranks, and a number of them handed over their arms (III, p. 44).

Following Gandhi's arrest the storm burst.

Gandhi's arrest led to hartals and strikes all over India. Some fifty thousand textile workers downed tools in Bombay. Railway workers too joined the demonstration. There was a mammoth procession impressive enough to induce the police to retire from the scene. The cloth merchants decided on a six-day hartal. In Poona, where Gandhi was interned, resignations from honorary offices and from services were announced at frequent intervals.

The revolutionary zeal was at its zenith. In Sholapur, the people held possession of the town for a week, replacing the police and establishing their own rule, until the martial law was proclaimed. There was trouble in Mymensingh, Calcutta, Karachi, Lucknow, Multan, Delhi, Rawalpindi, Mardan and Peshawar. Troops, aeroplanes, tanks, guns and ammunition were brought on the scene and freely used in

> the North-West Frontier Province. In June, 500 tons of bombs were dropped over the Pathans but their spirit remained uncrushed. The number of Red Shirts increased from a couple of hundreds to 80,000. Repression in the Punjab gave birth to the Ahrar Party, a spirited Muslim organization (III, p. 49).

However, while the people were thus magnificently responding to the call of the Congress, its leadership headed by Gandhi was doing its best to divert their enthusiasm and militancy to channels which were safe for the bourgeoisie. This they did in several ways.

Firstly, though they were forced to accept the immediate objective of complete independence, in actual practice, they gave it up before the ink was dry on the Independence Pledge. In his comments on the Viceroy's announcement, Gandhi said that he was prepared to 'put off civil disobedience if Britain would grant the substance, if not the outward form, of self-government.' He demanded eleven things: total prohibition; restoration of the exchange rate to 1*s.* 4*d.*; 50 per cent reduction of land revenue; reduction of military expenditure by at least 50 per cent to begin with; reduction of civil services salaries by half; a protective tariff against foreign cloth; enactment of a coastal reservation bill; discharge of all political prisoners, not condemned for murder or attempted murder; abolition or control of the C.I.D.; and issue of licences for fire-arms for self-defence, subject to popular control.

Enumerating these eleven points, Gandhi said: 'Let the Viceroy satisfy us with regard to thes very simple but vital needs of India. He will then hear no talk of civil disobedience.'

Secondly, despite the talk of mass civil disobedience, they tried to restrict the scope of direct action to a limited number of satyagrahis. Gandhi said addressing the students of Gujarat Vidyapith:

> We rely not on numerical strength, but on the strength of character, and the civil disobedience resolution was moved

> more because I had faith in a few men sacrificing themselves for the cause than in the number of men coming forward in response to the call (III, p. 2).

Thirdly, precisely in order to restrict the scope of the movement, they refrained from incorporating the demands of the millions of workers, peasants and other sections of the toiling people in the charter of demands which, according to Gandhi, was 'the substance of independence.' The above noted eleven points, for example, do not include anything which the workers or peasants demand from their employers, landlords and usurers. The only demand which was of direct interest to the peasants was the 50 per cent reduction in land revenue. Such questions as rent reduction, moratorium on debts, stoppage of evictions, adequate wages and salaries for the workers and employees, etc., were not considered.

It is true that a year later at the Karachi Congress the Congress leaders accepted many of the demands of the toiling people in the well-known resolution on fundamental rights. Acceptance of such demands as living wage for industrial workers, limited hours of work, healthy conditions of work, protection against the economic consequences of old age, sickness and unemployment, substantial reduction in agricultural rent or revenues paid by the peasantry and, in case of uneconomic holdings, exemption from rent for such period as may be necessary, were incorporated in the Congress programme. It should, however, be noted that, in his speech moving the resolution, Gandhi said:

> *This resolution is meant for those who are not legislators, who are not interested in the intricate questions of constitution, and who will not take an active part in the administration of the country. It is meant to indicate to the poor inarticulate Indians the broad features of Swaraj or Ram Raj.* Before my march to Dandi, I had included some of these features in my eleven points. These have been made more comprehensive. They are now presented to you in a separate resolution. They were

> advisedly omitted from the main resolution because that would have made the mandate for the delegation burdensome (III, pp. 112–13. emphasis added).

In other words, the Karachi programme was formulated with a two-fold purpose: firstly, to enable the Congress leadership to rouse the toiling people and delude them with the idea that the Congress was fighting for these demands of theirs; secondly, to use the strength of popular support thus acquired to secure from the British government the demands incorporated in the eleven points.

Above all, the adoption of the immediate objective of complete independence, or the decision to launch mass civil disobedience, did not make the slightest change in the technique which Gandhi had evolved ever since the days of the South African satyagraha—the technique of negotiations with the imperialists backed by controlled mass action. In words as well as in action, he made it repeatedly clear that his primary objective was to have a settlement with the British government. He stated in his well-known letter to the Viceroy before launching the civil disobedience movement:

> Conversion of a nation that has consciously or unconsciously preyed upon another, far more numerous, far more ancient, and no less cultured than itself, is worth any amount of risk.
>
> I have deliberately used the word conversion. For, my ambition is no less than to convert the British people through non-violence, and thus make them see the wrong they have done to India (III, p. 22).

It was these three features of the mass civil disobedience movement, launched by the Congress under Gandhi's leadership in 1930, that was sought to be cleverly used by the British government through its two viceroys—Lord Irwin and Lord Willingdon. The tactics adopted by the British imperialists in 1930–32 may be briefly summed up thus:

To begin with, they adopted what is commonly known as

the 'dual policy': the policy of repression against the people and negotiations with the leaders. It was this dual policy that enabled them to make the Congress leadership agree to call off the civil disobedience movement in 1931, and to send their representative to the second Round Table Conference.

Having made the Congress agree to withdraw the civil disobedience movement and to participate in the Round Table Conference, they adopted the policy of repression in India, combined with such manoeuvres among the non-Congress delegates at the Round Table Conference as would isolate the Congress representative. This enabled the British government to make out to the world that there was a very complicated problem of constitutional reform in India which the Indian leaders were not able to solve and that, therefore, the British government itself had to give its solution—what was called the communal award.

Having thus isolated the Congress at the Round Table conference and having 'exposed' the incapacity of the Congress to solve 'intricate' questions of constitutional reforms, the imperialist rulers launched a direct and ferocious attack on the Congress. By the time Gandhi came back from the Round Table Conference, provinces like UP and North-West Frontier Province had already come under ordinance rule and several top leaders of the Congress, including Jawaharlal Nehru, had already been clapped into jail. All the attempts that Gandhi made to negotiate with the Viceroy and to settle the issues of conflict proved abortive. When Gandhi and the Congress Working Committee did, therefore, decide to end the state of truce arrived at in March 1931 and to resume civil disobedience, the whole country was made the victim of an unheard-of state of repression.

These tactics of the imperialists were quite naturally sought to be combated by the leadership of the Congress. The way this was done is an unmistakable indication of how the philosophy and technique of Gandhism worked in actual practice.

In the stage of preparation for and launching of civil disobedience in the form of defiance of the Salt Laws, they tried to rouse the anti-imperialist consciousness in people but also tried to temper it with the insistence on non-violence, including the philosophy of 'converting' the British imperialists. The well-known Independence Pledge asserted that 'the British government has ruined India economically, politically, culturally and spiritually. . . . We hold it to be a crime against man and God to submit any longer to a rule that has caused this four-fold disaster to our country.' It added, 'We recognize however that the most effective way of gaining our freedom is not through violence.'

It was in keeping with this that the very eleven points were drafted: they were directed against British exploitation and would, therefore, rally all sections of the people including the bourgeoisie. But they were not directed against the Indian exploiters and would, therefore, not lead to any outbreak of what is known as 'mob violence.'

When this stage was over and *a new stage of negotiations with the British government* opened, they used all the avenues of negotiation in order to bring about such a settlement as would strengthen the economic and political position of the bourgeoisie vis-à-vis the British government. The terms on the basis of which Gandhi and the two Nehrus said they were prepared to call off the civil disobedience movement were that (a) India's right to secede at will from the British empire should be recognized in so many words; (b) a completely national government responsible to the Indian people should have control and should realize all the eleven points raised in Gandhi's letter to the Viceroy; and (c) India should have the right to refer to an independent tribunal British claims, concessions and the like, including the so-called public dept of India.

However, when it was found that a settlement on such terms was impossible, they agreed to accept a truce which strengthened the political and organizational position of the Congress in the country. The very fact that the mighty British government negotiated with the Congress and came to a written agreement with its representative; that such a settlement included provisions which partially conceded the demands of the Congress (like the permission to manufacture salt in certain areas); that the overwhelming majority of political prisoners were released—these were sufficient to strengthen the Congress and enable it to carry on its struggle for independence.

They therefore tried zealously to safeguard the gains secured by them through the truce and told the people that they had accepted the terms of truce only because it would enable them to still further strengthen the struggle for independence. Since, however, this was a position which the bureaucrats did not like, there were interminable conflicts between the Congress and the bureaucrats on such issues as release of political prisoners, enforcement of state laws, collection of land revenue, etc.

On every one of these issues, the Congress leadership tried its utmost to secure the redressal of grievances and always held out the threat that they would not send their representative to the second Round Table Conference if the truce terms were not strictly implemented by the government. It was because some concessions were made from the side of the government that they ultimately allowed Gandhi to go and attend the Round Table Conference.

Both at the second Round Table conference as well as later, they sought to combat the communal disruption organized by the British by a policy of concessions to the Muslims and certain other minorities. It was, however, found that the disruption at the second Round Table conference had laid the basis for the British government to start a frontal attack on the Congress. This naturally provoked it to resume direct action. But no sooner had the second civil disobedience movement started than the most farsighted of them, Gandhi, started evolving new tactics.

It was on 4 January 1932 that Gandhi was arrested. By 11 March, however, he had come to the conclusion that there was something more important for him than the effective conduct of the civil disobedience movement for securing complete independence. In a letter to the secretary of state dated 11 March, he wrote:

> You will perhaps recollect that at the end of my speech at the Round Table conference when the minorities' claim was

> presented, I had said that I should resist with my life the grant of separate electorate to the depressed classes. This was not said in the heat of the moment or by way of rhetoric. It was meant to be a serious statement (III, p. 195).

The communal award given by the British prime minister, he said, (according to which separate electorates were to be given to the depressed classes) would therefore force him to undertake a fast unto death.

That letter was the beginning of a process of the Congress slowly disengaging itself from the mass civil disobedience movement and adopting a new programme of parliamentary struggle on the one hand, and constructive programme on the other. on the rejection of his demand by the British government and the final acceptance and giving the communal award Gandhi undertook a fast unto death.

This fast led to a conference of Congress and non-Congress leaders, including leaders of the depressed classes, which came to an agreement enabling an amendment to be passed to the communal award in relation to the depressed classes.

As one of the provisions of the agreement was a countrywide mass campaign for the eradication of untouchability and for the amelioration of the condition of the depressed class, Gandhi was allowed to carry on Harijan work from inside jail. This diverted the energy of a large number of Congressmen outside jail from the job of organizing the civil disobedience movement into that of organizing Harijan welfare work.

As Gandhi said that he was not entirely satisfied with the progress of Harijan work, he undertook a 21-days' fast in May 1933 as a measure of self-purification. This led to his release from jail, an event which he used to advise the then acting-president of the Congress to suspend civil disobedience.

Since, however, these gestures of Gandhi and the acting-president of the Congress did not have the desired effect of making the government relax its policy of repression, Gandhi advised the resumption of civil disobedience, but not on a mass scale. He put restrictions on the manner in which it was to be conducted. He himself offered individual civil disobedience and the whole country was put on the rails of individual, as opposed to mass, civil disobedience.

Again, Gandhi undertook a fast in jail since the government refused this time to give him facilities to carry on Harijan work from inside jail. He had once more to be released, since, at one stage, his physical condition became really serious. On release, he said that he was going to work exclusively for the Harijan cause and keep away completely from political work.

The last few months of 1933 and the beginning of 1934 were used by Gandhi for an intensive tour of the country for the ostensible purpose of collecting funds for Harijan work. However, this was utilized by him and the other leaders of the Congress who were outside jail to have informal consultations on the future of civil disobedience. Some of the Congress leaders had already met among themselves and were thinking of organizing a Swaraj Party. They naturally sought Gandhi's advice. The result of these confabulations was that on 7 April 1934 Gandhi issued a statement in which he said:

> . . . . I must advise all Congressmen to suspend civil resistance for Swaraj, as distinguished from the specific grievances. They should leave it to me alone. It should be resumed by others in my lifetime, only under my direction, unless one arises claiming to know the scene better than I do and inspires confidence. I express this opinion as the author and initiator of satyagraha. Henceforth, therefore, those who have been impelled to civil resistance for Swaraj under my advice directly given or indirectly inferred, will please desist from civil resistance (III, p. 319).

This statement of Gandhi was followed by a statement from the government which assured the Congress that there would be 'no obstacle to a meeting of the AICC or, if Congress leaders so prefer, of the Indian National Congress for the purpose of ratifying the statement of policy recently made by Mr. Gandhi and calling off civil disobedience.'

The stage was thus set for the May meeting of the AICC which ratified Gandhi's statement withdrawing civil disobedience and decided to participate in the forthcoming elections to the central legislature.

Retirement

The very narration of these events will inevitably raise the question: why did Gandhi act in this manner? Why is it that, at the very time when the country was witnessing a big mass action directed against the national enemy, the supreme leader of that action preferred to pay attention to a relatively minor issue (the issue of the untouchables' position in the social and state structure) and make it the basis for a social reform, rather than a political mass movement? Why is it that he took the first available opportunity to advise the suspension of mass civil disobedience?

These are questions for which no answer can be found if one is to base oneself on Gandhi's pronouncements on satyagraha. The only contingency in which his theory of satyagraha visualized the withdrawal of mass action for a just cause was when that action had taken, or was in danger of taking 'violent' forms. It was this danger that Gandhi had stressed as the reason for the suspension of the movement in 1922. Such a contingency did not exist in 1932. Despite the highly provocative and brutal actions perpetrated by foreign rulers, the satyagrahis remained as peaceful and non-violent as Gandhi had asked them to be.

The thousands of young men and women satyagrahis had scrupulously observed all of Gandhi's instructions. Thus it came as a blow to them when they learned of Gandhi's decision to go on a fast on the question of separate electorates for the untouchables; still more severe was the shock when they subsequently learned that he had decided to devote his whole time and energy to the cause of Harijan uplift. They felt betrayed and angry when they saw the foremost leader of the anti-imperialist *political* action devoting himself, and asking his followers to devote themselves, to this relatively minor *social issue.*

Why did Gandhi decide on this apparently reckless change in tactics and thereby invite the acute dissatisfaction of thousands of his followers? Was it because he was 'more concerned with social reform than political struggles,' as is asserted by some people? The answer is 'No.' Gandhi was, above all, the astute political leader of a class—the bourgeoisie— in whose class interests he always acted. His September 1932 fast and the subsequent activity on the ostensibly *social* issue of Harijan uplift was part and parcel of his carefully worked out *tactics* with a view to meeting a concrete *political situation.*

Let us recall, in this connection, how the 1932 struggle came to be launched. The second Round Table Conference, at which Gandhi represented the Congress, ended in a break between the Congress and the British government. There was no other way open for a self-respecting national organization like the Congress, under these circumstances, than to launch mass action. The government for its part was determined on a showdown with the Congress and took adequate steps to see that the story of 1930–31 (Congress-government negotiations) was not repeated. In other words, the 1932 struggle was something which had been forced on Gandhi and his colleagues of the Congress Working Committee.

Gandhi was of opinion that, if this situation was allowed to continue, then the government would be able to have its way: frame a constitution on the lines on which it wanted. This constitution would be utilized by the non-Congress parties, including the communal ones, to weaken the Congress, who in their turn, would be utilized by the British to deny the national demand. He wanted to prevent this contingency and, therefore, to seek all possible ways of opening negotiations with the British, and, naturally, of withdrawing the civil disobedience movement.

It was to this end that he chose an issue which was at once of a social as well as of a political character—separate or joint electorates for the untouchables. While this gave him an opportunity to appear before the people and do something for social reform, it also gave an opening for negotiations with the government on one aspect of constitutional reform. The government, however, took him at his word, took his interest in the uplift of the untouchables as a matter of pure social reform and refused to open negotiations on the political question. Gandhi, for his part, used even this little opportunity to strengthen his contact with his colleagues and the people in general.

Subsequent events, however, proved that his interest in the cause of Harijan welfare was not merely social. At the first opportunity after coming out of jail (in May 1933) he used his authority over the Congress president to withdraw mass civil disobedience. But, even this opening for negotiations on the political issue was turned down by the British who wanted nothing but total surrender from the Congress. He had, therefore, to preserve his own, as well as the organization's self-respect by launching civil disobedience, though not on a mass scale. Once again, however, he took the first opportunity to give a hint to the government by announcing his decision to keep silent on political issues for a year.

His interest in the Harijan cause and the activities flowing therefrom should be considered as nothing but an effort on his part to disengage the Congress from the situation in which it had been placed following its break with the government. It was an effort to find points of contact with the British, pursue the negotiations on constitutional reforms started and temporarily broken at the second Round Table Conference, and to reorganize the Congress with a view to enabling it to meet this new situation.

That is precisely why, unlike in 1922 when even such moderate right-wing leaders as Motilal Nehru protested against Gandhi's action in suspending civil disobedience, the 1934 advice of Gandhi on the withdrawal of the movement was heartily endorsed by the entire right-wing leadership of the Congress. Furthermore, unlike the 1920s when the Congress leadership was split into the Swarajists and the no-changers, the 1930s saw an almost complete unanimity in the leadership on the question of parliamentary work. Gandhi himself stated in 1934 that 'parliamentary mentality has come to stay.' The entire right-wing leadership of the Congress was one in its view that the constitution that was then being drafted was the biggest political issue and that any negative attitude towards it would be dangerous. Hence, it was not a Swaraj Party outside the

Congress as in the 1920s, but the All India Congress Committee itself that appointed a parliamentary board of its own, which was to guide Congress activities with regard to the elections.

While there was thus an almost complete unanimity in the leadership of the Congress regarding the tactics that should be pursued, the Congress as an organization was by no means united. A process of intense discussion had started in the ranks of the Congress. The tactics pursued by Gandhi ever since his September 1932 fast were being very seriously challenged. So were the activities of certain right-wing leaders who had taken the initiative for the formation of the Swaraj Party, subjected to sharp criticism. Never before was discontent against the policies of the Congress leadership so widespread and so acute as in 1933–34. The extent to which this had gone may be gauged from a letter which Jawaharlal Nehru wrote to Gandhi in 1934. He wrote:

> And so the flag of Indian freedom was entrusted with all pomp and circumstance to those who had actually hauled it down at the height of our national struggle at the bidding of the enemy; to those who had proclaimed from the house-tops that they had given up politics—for politics were unsafe then—but who emerged with a jump to the front ranks when politics became safe.
>
> And what of the ideals they set forth before them, speaking as they did on behalf of the Congress and the nation? A pitiful hotchpotch, avoiding real issues, toning down, as far as they dared, even the political objective of the Congress, expressing a tender solicitude for every vested interest, bowing down to many a declared enemy of freedom, but showing great truculence and courage in facing the advanced and fighting elements in the Congress ranks (III, p. 381).

As for the 1934 decision on the withdrawal of the movement and on the adoption of the parliamentary programme, the news of it came to Nehru 'with such a stab of pain, I felt the chords of allegience that had bound me to him for many years had snapped.'

Tendulkar adds, 'this was the reaction of many Congressmen.'

The opposition of rank and file Congressmen, however, did not take the form of opposition to the parliamentary programme as such. Like the leadership, they too realized the importance of using parliamentary institutions as weapons in the struggle for freedom. They had no more fascination for the programme of boycott of legislatures than the leaders. But the question was: what are the parliamentary institutions to be used for? Are they to be used as avenues for reopening negotiations with the British, or are they to be used as the means of further strengthening the anti-imperialist mass movement? Again, is the utilization of parliamentary institutions to become the main, if not the sole, means of strengthening the anti-imperialist movement, or is it to be subordinated to the mobilization of the people, particularly of the workers, peasants and the middle classes, in uncompromising struggle against imperialism and its agents? These were the questions which were agitating tens of thousands of ordinary Congressmen.

These developments inside the Congress organization, together with such major developments in the national and international fields as the unprecedented crisis of the capitalist system (1929–33 world economic crisis), the successful implementation of the First Five Year Plan in the Soviet Union, the rise of Nazism in Germany and similar forces in several capitalist countries, the heroic defence of the cause of communism by the communists in the Meerut Conspiracy Case, etc., attracted thousands of revolutionary youth towards the communist ideology.

It was this that facilitated the slow but sure strengthening of the various communist groups in the country and their joining together to form the first all India centre of the Communist Party of India towards the end of 1933. A few months after the formation of the all India centre, the Government of India came down with its heavy hand and declared the Party illegal. This action did hamper the expansion and strengthening of the CPI, although it could not prevent the thousands of young anti-imperialists, disillusioned with Gandhian leadership, from thinking on the more radical lines of socialism. The Congressmen who thought on these lines got together and decided to form the Congress Socialist Party at a conference held in May 1934.

It was the realization that the new socialist trend growing inside the Congress had a powerful spokesman in Jawaharlal Nehru that led Gandhi towards the adoption of a new programme—a programme that was in the beginning shocking to the mass of Congressmen but which later on proved to be of enormous help to those Congressmen who wanted to fight the new radical trends in the Congress.

In September 1934, Gandhi wrote to Sardar Patel:

> Then there is the growing group of socialists. Jawaharlal is their undisputed leader. I know pretty well what he wants and stands for . . . The socialist group represents his views more or less, though probably their mode of execution is not exactly his. That group is bound to grow in influence and importance. . . . I have fundamental differences with them on the programme published in their authorized pamphlets. But I would not, by reason of the moral pressure I may be able to exert, suppress the spread of the ideas propounded in their literature. My remaining in the Congress would amount to the exercise of such pressure (III, pp. 387–88).

Gandhi's alternative was to retire from the Congress. Explaining this proposal, he issued a long statement on 17 September 1934 in the course of which he outlined the main points of difference between him and what he termed the 'intelligentsia.' He reaffirmed his faith in non-violence as a creed, and not as a policy, as in the case of the mass of Congressmen. He reiterated his faith in the spinning wheel and khadi. He expressed his differences with what he called the 'parliamentary party,' though, as in the case of the socialists, he would not exert his moral pressure against their growth. Hence the feeling that he required 'complete detachment and absolute freedom of action' in order to pursue the 'experiment in satyagraha' to which his whole life was dedicated.

The proposed retirement of Gandhi from the Congress naturally raised intense discussion. The one topic which was uppermost in the minds of the delegates who assembled at Bombay in October for the all India session was Gandhi's retirement. Repeated appeals were made to him to reconsider his decision but he remained adamant. The session passed a resolution reiterating its 'confidence in the leadership of Mahatma Gandhi.' It stated, further on, that the Congress

> is emphatically of opinion that he should reconsider his decision to retire from the Congress. But inasmuch as efforts to persuade him in that behalf have failed, this Congress, while reluctantly accepting his decision, places on record its deep sense of gratitude for the unique services rendered by him to the nation and notes, with satisfaction, his assurance that his advice and his guidance will be available to the Congress whenever necessary (III, p. 372).

His retirement from the Congress was stated to be for the double purpose of allowing him to devote his entire time and energy to the constructive programme, and to enable the parliamentarians, the socialists and other groups inside the Congress to carry on their activities without the danger of his moral pressure being exerted on them. He therefore made it a point to give no public statements or speeches on any controversial political subject. The columns of the *Harijan*, in which he continuously wrote; the innumerable speeches which he delivered during his countrywide tours; the press interviews that he frequently gave and the bulk of his correspondence were all related to such subjects as khadi, village industries, untouchability, cleanliness, cow protection, birth control, and any number of other subjects which bore no relation to current political issues.

In reality, however, he exerted his influence in the political life of the Congress, since he was available at all times for 'consultation' by Congressmen. The leading members of the Working Committee rushed to him for advice on all important political questions. His retirement from the Congress, therefore, was by no means retirement from political activity. This he made clear in the course of discussions which he had with his devoted colleagues and followers. For example, at a meeting of the Gandhi Seva Sangh held in February 1936, he said:

> I see that there is a tendency to believe that these programmes (constructive and political) are mutually exclusive or antagonistic. Much of our misunderstanding arises out of this belief. The worker in the constructive field looks down upon the political programme and vice versa. But really there is no such opposition. I had thought that it was clear by now to every worker that there was no absolute division between the so-called political and the so-called constructive programmes. In our method of work there are no water-tight compartments (IV, p. 66).

In all his speeches and writings, he emphasized the point that the Harijan, village industries and other parts of the constructive programme were integral parts of his programme of non-violent struggle for the establishment of a free India. That being so, there was no question of his retiring from politics.

While thus tendering advice to, and striving to mould the policies of the Congress leadership, Gandhi also tried to advise and influence the leaders of the rising Congress Socialist Party. In a letter which he wrote to Acharya Narendra Deva, he advised the socialists to consult Jawaharlal Nehru.

> I feel sure that if he was in our midst [Nehru was at that time in jail], he would have hastened slowly. I suggest your presenting the country with practical socialism in keeping with Indian conditions, instead of scientific socialism as your programme has been called. I am glad that the programme

> you have given me is but a draft, though prepared by an influential committee appointed for the purpose. It would be wise, if when you settle your programme finally, you will associate with you men who have socialist leanings and have experience of actual conditions (III, Photostat, p. 344).

This advice to the Congress socialists to consider Jawaharlal Nehru as their leader and act under his guidance was no accident, nor was it merely an expression of his personal regard for Nehru. It was part and parcel of a definite policy which Gandhi was pursuing. It will be useful, in this connection, to recall that, at the time when he had recommended the election of Jawaharlal Nehru for the presidency of the Lahore Congress, he had told the militant youth of the country that Nehru's election should be considered as a tribute to their services. He had compared them with steam 'which becomes a mighty power only when it allows itself to be imprisoned in a strong little reservoir and produces tremendous motion,' adding, 'even so should the youth of the country of their free will allow their inexhaustible energy to be imprisoned, controlled and set free in strictly measured and required quantities.' In other words, he looked upon Nehru as the instrument through which the Congress leadership could direct the patriotism and self-sacrificing spirit of the youth of the country into 'proper channels.' This had worked in 1930–32, Gandhi reasoned—it might work in the new period as well.

His strategy, therefore, was to strengthen the forces of the right inside the Congress on the one hand and to allow the leadership of Jawaharlal Nehru on the other, while he himself remained in the background offering advice and influencing the policies of both the right and the left. This, in essence, was the meaning of his retirement from active Congress leadership.

United Front

This was a strategy which was fully in keeping with the political requirements of the right-wing leadership of the Congress. Faced as they were with the challenge of the British Government in the form of the new constitution that was soon to be forced on the people, the Congress leadership could not afford to have any deep division inside the organization. Differences between the right and the left, differences between such social philosophies as Gandhism, modern socialism and bourgeois parliamentarianism, differences on social and religious questions—all these had to be adjusted with a view to enabling the Congress as an organization to offer a united front against the national enemy. Accommodating the socialists and other left forces while preserving the dominant position of the parliamentarians and other rightists was thus of supreme importance for the right-wing Congress leadership.

It was, however, not only a question of accommodating the socialists and other leftists inside the Congress. Something more was needed. The forces of the left had to be put in such a position that the large mass of the working people and the growing ranks of socialist-minded and other radical youth were given the confidence that the Congress was pursuing a genuine policy of radical anti-imperialism. It was this consideration that made the Congress leadership adopt the same technique as they did in 1929—put the leader of the left at the head of the organization. Just as in 1929, so also in 1936, Nehru was elected president of the Congress. What is more, when his term was over and a new president had to be elected in 1937, he was re-elected. As if two successive terms for Nehru were not enough, the presidency of the Congress was then given to another leader of the left: Subhas Chandra Bose was elected to succeed Nehru in 1938. During all these terms of leftist presidents of the Congress, the Congress Working Committee included members of the Congress Socialist

Party and other leftists. How the leaders of the right looked upon this left orientation of the Congress was explained by Sardar Patel in 1936, when his name was proposed for the presidency and he withdrew in favour of Nehru:

> My withdrawal should not be taken to mean that I endorse all the views Jawaharlal stands for. Indeed, Congressmen know that, on some vital matters, my views are in conflict with those held by Jawaharlal. . . . There may be a sharp division of opinion between Jawaharlal and myself, or rather among Congressmen. We know him to be too loyal to the Congress to disregard the decision of the majority, assuming that the latter lays down a policy repugnant to him. He is the chairman of our well-built organization. The Congress does not part with its powers by electing any individual, no matter who he is. I ask the delegates to plumb for Jawaharlal as being the best person to represent the nation and guide in right channel the different forces that are at work in the country (IV, p. 132).

This indeed was a policy which paid rich dividends, Nehru's two-year term of presidency (1936–38), the election manifesto and the agrarian programme drafted under his guidance and with the collaboration of the socialists, the hurricane tour that Nehru undertook for the popularization of the two documents, the selfless activity of tens of thousands of left-minded youth who were roused by the radical slogans popularized by Nehru—these were a very big factor in mobilizing millions of people behind the Congress and against reactionary forces in the 1937 general elections. The fact that communal and other reactionary forces were routed and the Congress came out with comfortable majorities in 7 out of 11 provinces was mainly due to this leftist orientation of the Congress agitation.

This leftist orientation of the Congress also helped its leadership in the post-election months when serious differences arose between the Congress and the British government. The new constitution under which elections had taken place and new legislatures formed, conferred extremely wide powers on provincial governors which, if exercised, would make a mockery of the elected legislatures and ministries responsible to them. The Congress leadership, therefore, wanted an assurance from the British that these powers would not be used, as a condition precedent to the acceptance of ministries in those provinces where it had been returned in a majority. The British were not prepared to give this assurance. There was, therefore, a deadlock on the question; a breakdown of the entire constitution at the very time when it was being brought into force was feared.

It was only the solid unity of the Congress organization—a unity that made it clear to the British that non-acceptance of the Congress demands would lead to serious consequences—that forced them to retreat from the original position. At the end of a prolonged public debate, in which the secretary of state for India, Lord Zetland, spoke for the British government and Gandhi for the Congress (incidentally, the role played by Gandhi in this controversy shows the real character of his retirement from Congress leadership), the Congress and the British came to an arrangement which was not entirely satisfactory from the national point of view and which was criticized by radical elements from within the Congress, yet enabled the Congress to come to a decision in favour of forming ministries.

This decision changed Gandhi's method of working. No more was he going to stick to the earlier decision of confining his activities to the constructive programme alone. On 17 July 1937, he wrote in the *Harijan*:

> Since the Working Committee and other Congressmen have allowed themselves to be influenced by my opinion on office acceptance issue, it is perhaps due to the public for me to explain my conception of office acceptance and what is possible to do in terms of the Congress election manifesto. I need offer no apology for crossing the self-imposed limit in the conduct of *Harijan*. The reason is obvious. The

> Government of India Act is universally regarded as wholly unsatisfactory for achieving India's freedom. But it is possible to construe it as an attempt, however limited and feeble, to replace the rule of the sword by the rule of the majority. The creation of the big electorate of three crores of men and women and the placing of wide powers in their hands cannot be described by any other name. Underlying it is the hope that what has been imposed upon us we shall get to like, that is, we shall really regard our exploitation as a blessing in the end. The hope may be frustrated, if the representatives of the thirty million voters have a faith of their own and are intelligent enough to use the powers—including the holding of offices—placed in their hands, for the purpose of thwarting the assumed intention of the framers of the Act. And this can be easily done by lawfully using the Act in a manner not expected by them and by refraining from using it in the way intended by them (IV, p. 207).

This was the beginning of a new phase in Gandhi's leadership of the Congress organization. Still continuing to remain formally outside the organization, he nevertheless became the dominant force in guiding the various Congress ministries. Week after week, he wrote in the *Harijan* by way of advising the ministries as to how they should conduct themselves and what they should do under various circumstances. Tendulkar remarks that the newspapers described his writings in those days as the 'instrument of instructions.' Through the columns of the *Harijan*, as well as through his personal advice to the ministers and other Congress leaders, Gandhi laid down the policy on such questions as prohibition, education, taxation, etc. It was again he who effectively intervened in all those cases where the Congress ministers in the provinces had to, and did come in conflict with the governors or the Viceroy. For example, it was he who acted as the political spokesman of the Congress in the ministerial conflicts which developed on the issue of release of political prisoners in Bihar and UP. It was again because of his intervention that the threatened crisis in Orissa was averted when conflict arose over the appointment of a civilian official subordinate to the ministry as the governor.

However, the very unity of the left and the right in a common organization at whose head stood the leader of the left enormously strengthened the forces of the left. Ideas of socialism, of militant and uncompromising anti-imperialism, of anti-landlord and anti-capitalist struggles, of unity and solidarity with the anti-imperialist, anti-fascist and peace forces through out the world—these began to grip the people on a scale never before thought possible. Organizations of the working class, the peasantry, the students and youth and other sections of the people, as well as the Congress socialists, the communists and other parties and elements which spoke in the name of scientific socialism, began to grow at an unprecedented pace. The millions of common people in the so-called 'Indian States' were awakened to a new sense of their rights and embarked on struggles for democratic constitutions in their respective States.

All these were, of course, partly the result of developments in the international field—the growing might of the Soviet Union, the success of anti-fascist forces in Europe, the epic battles of the anti-fascist and national-liberation forces in Spain, China and Abyssinia, etc. The reflection of this new consciousness, even inside the Congress leadership, was a powerful factor in the consolidation of the new forces of radical anti-imperialism and socialism.

Office Acceptance and After

While the right-wing leadership did not very much bother itself with this growth of the left forces in the first stage of the anti-imperialist united front—the stage in which it was preparing itself to meet the challenge of the British and winning a resounding electoral victory—it found this new situation extremely inconvenient after it had won its victory over the British. With the acceptance of office by Congressmen in several provinces, says Tendulkar,

> New problems arose and internal conflicts which had so far been largely ideological, took new shape. No one, not even the opponents of the office acceptance, wanted to create trouble for Congress leaders, but there was a continuous attempt to bring pressure upon them by kisan demonstrations and strikes which embarrassed the Congress leaders greatly. In Bihar, the kisan movement came into conflict with the Congress organization. Elsewhere also, the high hopes that had been raised by the advent of the Congress leaders not being fulfilled, dissatisfaction arose (IV, p. 248).

This, therefore, was a situation in which the right-wing leadership of the Congress under Gandhi's guidance had to fight a two-pronged battle—against the British who were trying to force the extremely reactionary federal part of the Indian constitution and against the forces of the left which sought to use the election campaign and its results to push the Congress further to the left and to strengthen the forces of radical anti-imperialism. It was no more a question of uniting the right and the left in a common front against the national enemy, but of strengthening the position of the right both in relation to the left as well as in relation to the British. It was to meet this new situation that the Congress leadership under Gandhi worked out a strategy whose essential features may be summed up as follows:

Firstly, a concerted attack was launched on the working class and peasant organizations—attack in the form of police repression on the one hand and ideological attack on the other. Arrests, prosecutions, lathi-charges, even firings, began to be resorted to against working class and peasant organizations; sections of the Penal Code and the Criminal Procedure Code, which had become notorious through their use by the British against the Congress, began to be used by the Congress against the militant mass movement. All this was justified by Gandhi who defended the Congress ministries which resorted to them on the ground that

> Civil liberty is not criminal liberty. . . . In seven provinces, the Congress rules. It seems to be assumed by some persons that, in these provinces at least, individuals can say and do what they like. But so far as I know the Congress mind, it will not tolerate any such license (IV, pp. 248–49).

Secondly, they used the power that they had secured in the provinces to solve some of the problems which the nation was facing and thus to strengthen themselves in relation to the British and also to prove that they are quite capable of solving the main problems facing the country. It is significant that, not long after the assumption of ministerial office the Congress convened a conference of industrial ministers in the Congress provinces in order to evolve a common plan of economic development for the whole country. It was at this conference that a national planning committee with Jawaharlal Nehru as chairman and K.T. Shah as secretary was formed. This was the first significant effort on the part of the Congress to prepare a blueprint of the future independent India, the first effort to translate into practice the glorious vision that had been placed before the country by Sir M. Visweswarayya in his book on Indian planning.

Equally significant was the conference of educationists which worked out the broad outlines of the new educational system that the Congress would like to introduce in place of the imperialist system that was prevalent. (this was the beginning of what is today called basic education.) These efforts at 'constructive solutions' of the main problems of the nation, together with the 'firm' handling of the 'law and order situation' in the provinces, were supposed to prove that the Congress was not a party of 'irresponsible agitators,' but a 'responsible party' with a 'constructive programme' and the necessary 'administrative experience' to implement it.

Thirdly, they worked out a new approach towards the Indian States and their people's movements for democratic reforms.

The traditional approach of the Congress since the days of non-cooperation was one of 'non-interference in the internal affairs' of the States. This was justified on the ground that the national struggle was against the foreign oppressor and that the relation between the princes and people of the various Indian States was an internal affair, rather than part of the national struggle. That was why, even at the time when the 1928 Nehru Report was being prepared, the question of the Indian States was strictly kept out of the purview of the All Parties Committee's consideration.

It was, however, proved at the Round Table Conference that the British were using the position of the princes as the instrument with which to fight the Congress and its demand for Swaraj. This became all the more clear after the Government of India Act of 1935 became effective. The princes had a vital role to play in the scheme of Britain's bargaining with the Indian political parties on the question of the federal part of the constitution.

This anti-national use that was being made of the princes by the British made it necessary for the Congress leadership to adopt a new policy towards them and their autocratic rule. Furthermore, the new awakening that was seizing the entire Indian people in the wake of the growth of radical forces throughout the country was also having its impact on the people of the Indian States. Whether the Congress leadership like it or not, the people of the States were more and more coming forward and fighting for their democratic rights under the slogan of responsible government.

It was in this situation that the Haripura session of the

Congress, held in February 1938, adopted a new policy towards the States. According to this policy, the Congress changed its old 'non-interference in the internal affairs of the States' to encouraging the States' people to form their own organizations and fight for responsible government. It, however, continued its old policy in the sense that the Congress as such did not function as a political organization in the States. Gandhi himself started giving advice to the movements in one State after another. His chief lieutenants like Jamnalal Bajaj, Dr. Pattabhi Sitaramayya, etc., began to take active part in these struggles. Gandhi himself personally led the struggle in Rajkot.

Explaining this change in the Congress policy, he said:

> The policy of non-intervention by the Congress was, in my opinion, a perfect piece of statesmanship, when the people of the States were not awakened. That policy would be cowardice when there is all-round awakening among the people of the States and a determination to go through a long course of suffering for the vindication of their own rights (V, p. 30).

However, as in the case of other struggles led by him, here too, he found that the people, once roused into action, had a 'peculiar' tendency of going beyond the limits set by him. The States' people's movements of the latter half of the 1930s were more or less on the same level as the movement in 'British India' during the non-cooperation days. The spontaneous outburst of anger against oppressive rulers led to several incidents in State after State which Gandhi could not approve of. In Travancore, in Rajkot, in the Orissa States, etc., Gandhi discovered that his principles of satyagraha were not being strictly adhered to. Thus he came to evolve what is known as 'new technique' in relation to the States' people's struggles which he explained as follows:

> I am convinced direct negotiations should be opened with the authorities. Hitherto, the State Congress people have

> talked at the authorities and the latter at them. The result has been a widening of the gulf between them. It would not do for a satyagrahi to argue that the approach must be mutual. . . . The first and last work of a satyagrahi is always to seek an opportunity for an honourable approach. . . . If the leaders have active *ahimsa* in them, they must cultivate a belief in the perfect possibility and necessity of such approach. And if they have that belief, the way will surely be opened to them (V, pp. 152–53).

This, therefore, was an effort to show the princes that, while the Congress had the backing of the awakened people of the States, it was by no means anxious to see the people's movement develop on 'dangerous' lines; it was, on the other hand, anxious to control them and bring them on lines which would be 'safe' to the princes themselves. It was, in other words, a call to the princes to join the Congress against the British, rather than the other way.

Fourthly, while thus trying to control the forces of the left, to strengthen and consolidate the position it had won through the formation of ministries and to use the new awakening of the States' people in order to come to an understanding with the princes, the Congress leadership concentrated its attention on fighting the federal part of the constitution. It demanded that a new, democratically-elected constituent assembly should be convened in order to frame the future constitution of India. It was on this question of the future constitution, particularly its federal part, that the gulf between the Congress and the British was the widest.

It is interesting to note that it was on this very same question that the gulf became widest between the right and the left in the Congress as well. While opposing the federal part of the constitution and demanding a constituent assembly, Gandhi made it clear that he for one would be prepared to have negotiations with the British government. In an interview with Mr. Steel, the correspondent of the *New York Times*, Gandhi went to the extent of saying:

> If Dominion status could be so defined as to cover a case like India and if India could come to an honourable agreement with England, I would not quarrel about words. If British statesmen feel it convenient to use the word Dominion status about India rather than any other, in order to describe that honourable agreement, I will not quarrel.
>
> 'But,' rejoined Mr. Steel, 'there are elements in the Congress like Subhas Bose and his group who want absolute independence outside the British Empire.'
>
> 'It is only a question of terminology,' replied Gandhi. 'I will not admit any difference between Subhas Babu and myself on this point, though we may use different language' (V, p. 138).

Actually, however, the difference turned out to be far from one of terminology, but of basic approach to the main political organizational questions which the Congress had to face. There were differences which had undoubtedly existed since 1934 and had divided the Congress into its right and left wings. They, however, had been subordinated in 1934–38 to the necessity of having a united Congress at a time when it was fighting the first general elections under the 1935 constitution. It was to this end that the right-wing leaders of the Congress thought it necessary to have leftist presidents for three consecutive terms. However, after the formation of Congress ministries and after conflicts developed on a large-scale between the provincial ministries and rank-and-file Congressmen, the right-wing leadership thought that the phase of concessions to the left should end and a new phase of struggle against it begin. It was this that led to the Bose-Pattabhi contest for the presidency of the Tripuri session, a contest which was by no means a personal contest between the two, as can be seen from the actual course which the struggle took.

When Subhas Bose decided to Contest for a second term for presidency, Sardar Patel, Rajendra Prasad, Jamnalal Bajaj, Jairamdas Daulatram, Shankerrao Deo, Bhulabhai Desai and Kripalani issued a joint statement urging Subhas Bose to reconsider his decision and to allow Dr. Pattabhi Sitaramayya's election to be unanimous.

Subhas Bose's reply was:

> . . . . The attempt to set up a rightist candidate for the office of president is not without significance. It is widely believed that there is a prospect of a compromise on the federal scheme between the right wing of the Congress and the British government during the coming year. And consequently, the right-wing do not want a leftist president who may be a thorn in the way of compromise and may put obstacles in the path of negotiations. . . . it is imperative, in the circumstances, to have a Congress president who will be an anti-federationist to the core of his heart (V, p. 36).

Sardar Patel revealed in a statement issued on 25 January that the decision to set up Dr. Pattabhi as candidate was taken 'at the informal consultations at one stage or the other at which Maulana Azad, Jawaharlal Nehru, Rajendra Prasad, Bhulabhai Desai, Kripalani, Mahatma Gandhi and myself were present.'

Jawaharlal Nehru made a statement on 27 January in which he did not contradict Sardar Patel's statement regarding his participation in the above-mentioned informal consultations. He did not commit himself either for Pattabhi or for Subhas Bose, confining himself to 'regretting' that the presidential election controversy has taken an unfortunate turn. He made the categorical assertion that there was no question of a conflict over federation in this election as the Congress had definitely rejected this scheme. In other words, he took a stand of not directly and fully joining the rightists but virtually coming out against Subhas Bose's stand.

The result of this keenly-fought-out election contest was a rightist defeat, the voting being 1580 for Subhas Bose and 1375 for Pattabhi. On the announcement of the result, Gandhi wrote:

> Sri Subhas Bose has achieved a decisive victory over his

> opponent, Dr. Pattabhi Sitaramayya. I must confess that from the very beginning, I was decidedly against his re-election for reasons into which I reed not go. I do not subscribe to his facts or arguments in his manifestos. I think that his references to his colleagues were unjustified and unworthy. Nevertheless, I am glad of his victory. And since I was instrumental in inducing Dr. Pattabhi not to withdraw his name as a candidate, when Maulana Azad withdrew, the defeat is more mine than his (V, p. 30).

The right-wing leadership, however, was not prepared to take this defeat lying down. As a matter of fact, the very statement of Gandhi that he considered Subhas Bose's victory as his own defeat was used by them to mobilize public opinion to have the verdict of the Congress delegates reversed. Twelve members of the Working Committee—Sardar Patel, Maulana Azad, Rajendra Prasad, Mrs. Naidu, Bhulabhai Desai, Pattabhi Sitaramayya, Shankarrao Deo, Mehtab, Kripalani, Daulatram, Bajaj and Ghaffar Khan—resigned their membership of the Working Committee. In the course of a joint letter, 'believed to have been drafted by Gandhi,' they wrote:

> We feel that the time has come when the country should have a clear-cut policy not based on compromise between different incompatible groups of the Congress. It is but right, therefore, that you should select a homogeneous cabinet representing the views of the majority (V, p. 56).

Though not signing this joint letter of resignation, Nehru, too, resigned his membership of the Working Committee. In a separate letter he revealed that

> he had tried his best to bring about a compromise. He had pressed president Bose to withdraw the charges made by him in his pre-election statements with regard to the rightists

> compromising with the British government on the question of federation (V, p. 56).

The resignation of the thirteen members of the Working Committee, including Jawaharlal Nehru, was the beginning of the most serious internal crisis which the Congress had to face so far. That crisis was ultimately solved by the victory of the right.

The deep concern which the delegates showed at the Tripuri session was fully utilized by the right-wing leadership to have a resolution adopted, according to which Bose was to nominate a Working Committee for the ensuing year in accordance with the wishes of Gandhi.

However, when Bose approached Gandhi for his advice, he was told:

> Knowing your own views and knowing how most of the members differ in the fundamentals, it seems to me that if I give you the names it would be an imposition on you. I had argued this position at length in my letters to you. Nothing that has happened during these three days of closest conversation between us has altered my view. Such being the case, you are free to choose your own committee (V, pp. 102–3).

This attitude of Gandhi forced Bose to resign his presidency. Rajendra Prasad was elected in his place. He nominated a new Working Committee, consisting so exclusively of right-wing leaders that even Jawaharlal Nehru was kept out of it. One of the first steps taken by the new Working Committee was to convene a meeting of the AICC and to have two important resolutions adopted against the stout opposition of Subhas Bose, the socialists and other leftists. One of these resolutions prohibited Congressmen from offering, or organizing, any form of satyagraha in the administrative provinces of India without the sanction of the Provincial Congress Committee concerned. This was obviously intended to prevent Congressmen from participating in the innumerable peasant actions that were developing. Dr. Lohia argued:

> The people today do not regard your (Gandhi's) own programme in the ministerial action and constructive activities as wholly adequate; they are experimenting with such programmes as those of peasant action. These newer programmes entail an amount of local and isolated action, even during such times when there is no general satyagraha (V, p. 176).

Gandhi answered:

> I regret to have to say that, in most cases, the peasants are not being educated for non-violent action. . . . Indeed, what I see around me is not the preparation for a non-violent campaign but for an outbreak of violence, however unconscious or unintended it may be (V, pp. 177–8).

This resolution turned out to be the beginning of an intense organizational struggle. Subhas Bose and several other office-bearers and members of the executive committees of the Congress decided to observe 9 July as a 'day of protest' against the AICC resolution. The observance of this protest by them was considered by the Congress Working Committee which resolved 'that for his grave act of indiscipline, Sri Subhas Chandra Bose is declared disqualified as the president of the Bengal Provincial Congress committee for three years as from August 1939.'

This naturally led to an intense conflict between the right and the left. However, before it could lead to large-scale expulsions from the Congress, a far bigger crisis of world importance had developed. Hitler launched his attack on Poland. This was followed by Britain declaring war on Germany, and declaring India a party to this war. Countrywide resentment at this British action—making India a party to the war without consulting public opinion in India—reached an almost explosive stage when the Viceroy promulgated a number of ordinances since, according to him, 'a grave emergency' existed whereby 'the security of India is threatened by war.'

Conflict with Working Committee

The outbreak of the war very naturally raised the question whether Gandhi's attitude towards war had undergone change between the years of the first and Second World Wars. For, it will be recalled, being a votary of non-violence had not prevented him, in the period of the First World War, from acting as a recruiting sergeant for British imperialism. Would he do the same thing in the Second World War as well? This question was actually put to him by a well known Congressman to which he answered on 25 September 1939:

> My own personal reaction towards this war is one of greater horror than ever before. I was not so disconsolate before, as I am today. But the greater horror would prevent me today from becoming the self-appointed recruiting sergeant that I had become during the last war. And yet, strange as it may appear, my sympathies are wholly with the allies. Willy-nilly, this war is resolving into one of such democracy, as the West has evolved, and totalitarianism, as is typified in Herr Hitler (V, p. 207).

It would thus appear as if Gandhi's attitude towards Britain had not changed, as he would certainly like Britain to win, but he would not help the British through arms, because he had become more non-violent than in the days of the First World War. This however, is a picture which would be far from the truth.

Firstly, Gandhi's role as Britain's recruiting sergeant during the First World War was by no means a personal act, but an inseparable part of the policy then adopted by the entire Indian bourgeoisie. Barring a handful of revolutionaries like those of the Ghadr Party in America, and the so-called 'terrorists' of Bengal and some other provinces, the entire leadership of the national movement adopted the policy of helping Britain in the war but demanding of her that she should concede the national demand for responsible government.

Secondly, Gandhi himself was frank enough to admit that his own activities as recruiting agent were by no means divorced from the political objective of winning Swaraj. We have quoted in an earlier chapter how Gandhi had expressed the view that 'the easiest and straightest way to win Swaraj is to participate in the defence of the empire. If the empire perishes, with it perish our cherished aspirations. Some say that if we do not secure rights just now we would be cheated afterwards. This power acquired in defending the empire will be the power that can secure those rights.' He also added, 'if we are not prepared to make this sacrifice for the empire and Swaraj, it is no wonder if we are regarded as unworthy of it.'

Thirdly, the two decades that elapsed between the First and Second World War had seen such a tremendous strengthening of the Indian bourgeoisie that it secured provincial autonomy. The Congress itself was able to form its ministries in seven provinces. This strengthening of its position did by no means satisfy the bourgeoisie; the Congress therefore tried to further extend its power through mass pressure on the one hand and negotiations on the other. This was the strategy which the Congress worked out under Gandhi's leadership in the latter half of the 'thirties.

Naturally, therefore, the Congress attitude towards war was also governed by this strategy: while it was not prepared to give unconditional support to the British in their war efforts as it did during the First World War, the Congress leadership made it perfectly clear that they were prepared to give all possible forms of support to the British, provided their own demand for power at the centre was promised at least after the war.

This, however, was the position not only of the Congress but of the other parties and organizations under bourgeois or landlord leadership, such as the Muslim League, the Hindu Mahasabha, the Liberals, etc. These latter organizations had, of course, their own grievances and demands against the Congress; they were not prepared to support the Congress as against the British; but none of them was prepared to give that unconditional support to the British which their predecessors had done during the First World War.

It was this changed position of the bourgeoisie as a whole, and of the Congress in particular, that was reflected in Gandhi's own change of attitude. For, behind the so-called 'greater horror' towards war, which he developed since the First World War, lies the fact that the class which he represented has now become stronger than before, is now in a position to put pressure on the British by withholding support in the difficult days of war.

If we are to accept Tendulkar's story of the evolution of Gandhi's own and the Congress Working Committee's attitude towards war, there was a fundamental conflict between the two in the first few months of the Second World War. While Gandhi was for giving whatever support that the British needed without any conditions, the Working Committee was prepared to give support only under certain conditions; on the other hand, while the Working Committee was prepared to carry on such activities as recruitment of soldiers, etc., in support of the British, provided the latter satisfied the conditions laid down by the Congress, Gandhi was prepare to give only moral and non-violent support.

The basis of this difference between Gandhi and the Working Committee was ostensibly their different attitudes to the principle of non-violence. While the Working Committee was prepared to apply the principle of non-violence only in the struggle against the British government, while it was not prepared to bind itself to the adoption of only non-violent means in dealing with communal riots or goondaism or in resisting foreign invaders, Gandhi was insistent that all the problems of internal order and resistance to external attack should also be solved on the principles of *ahimsa.*

This difference in approach between Gandhi and the Working Committee led to a furious controversy and internal crisis in the Congress in the first few months of the war. Gandhi and his biographer would therefore have us believe that the closest followers and lieutenants of Gandhi including Sardar Patel, Rajagopalachari, etc., were coming into conflict with him because they were not prepared to go as far as Gandhi in the acceptance and application of the moral principle of nonviolence.

An examination of how this conflict developed would, however, show that, behind this conflict on an ostensibly moral question, lay the mundane question of what tactics should be adopted in dealing with the British. It will also be seen that there was a tacit division of labour between Gandhi on the one hand and the majority of the Congress Working Committee on the other. Consider, for example, the circumstances in which the conflict originally broke out, resolved temporarily, then again broke out in a more acute form and was once again resolved.

The conflict broke out in a mild form at the very first meeting of the Working Committee held after the outbreak of the war. This was the occasion on which, according to Gandhi, 'I was sorry to find myself alone in thinking that whatever support was to be given to the British should be given unconditionally' (V, p. 204). The circumstances in which the Working Committee refused to accept Gandhi's advice were that war had just broken out and that it was by no means clear how each side in the war and each country on the side of the non-fascist powers would react. The Working Committee, therefore, did not want to bind itself to a course of action which would weaken its position in any possible negotiations with the British. Such a weakening of its position would undoubtedly be the result both of offering unconditional support as well as of giving support—either conditional or unconditional—on a purely non-violent basis.

Subsequent developments, however, made it clear that the British were far from being ready for negotiations and settlement with the Congress on the basis laid down by the Congress. The pronouncements of the British Secretary of State, Lord Zetland, and the Indian Viceroy, Lord Linlithgow, made it clear that the demand of the Congress for a clear declaration of British policy as to whether democracy and self-determination would apply to India was being countered by the British imperialists with the claims made by the Muslim League, the Scheduled Castes Federation, the Liberals, the princes, etc. These pronouncements, said Gandhi, had 'the old familiar flavour'; they were relying on what he called the 'four pillars of British Indian empire—the European interests, the army, the princes and the communal divisions' (V, p. 202). It was also becoming clear that the use made by the British imperialists of the last of the 'four pillars,' the communal division, was becoming extremely uncomfortable for the Congress: the Muslim League particularly was getting increasingly strengthened and was creating serious obstacles in the path of the Congress along with certain other minorities.

All this convinced the Congress Working Committee that the British would not concede its demand unless greater pressure was brought to bear on them. The Committee, therefore, first called upon the Congress ministers in the provinces to resign; this was to be followed by other steps which were to prepare the country for 'all eventualities.' In these circumstances, Gandhi's stand on non-violence, his appeal to the British and other allied peoples not to meet Nazi militarism with counter-militarism, but to resist the Nazis with non-violent means, came in handy for the Working Committee. For, it served the purpose of whipping up the anti-war sentiment of the people which was already rising at a very fast rate an thus creating conditions in which the British rulers would realize that it was by no means easy for them to continue their war efforts.

In this period, therefore, not only was there no conflict between Gandhi and the Working Committee but the Working Committee itself asked the people in general and Congressmen in particular, to follow Gandhi's instructions in order to prepare themselves for the struggle. For the first time after the 1934 Bombay session, Gandhi addressed a session of the Congress at Ramgarh. The main resolution adopted at the session declared that, in view of the policy adopted by the British government, the Congress and those under its influence could not help in the prosecution of the war with men, money or material.

Gandhi in his speech explained at length his own ideas of

how the struggle against war was to be organized and conducted. Immediately following the Ramgarh session, Gandhi gave the slogan 'Every Congress Committee, A Satyagraha Committee.' He gave detailed instructions as to how the Congress committees and individual Congressmen should function as satyagrahis.

Soon, however, the international situation changed. Britain and her allies suffered a series of reverses at the hands of the Nazis in May-June 1940: the whole of Western Europe fell under the Nazi jackboots and there was great concern at the fate of Britain itself. There was a change of government in Britain, Churchill replacing Chamberlain. Questions began to be asked in India whether these developments would lead to any change in British policy towards India. Gandhi himself said: 'While the hourly butchery is going on in the West and peaceful homes are being destroyed. . . . I will leave no stone unturned to bring about a peaceful and honourable settlement of the present deadlock' (V, p. 349).

It was inevitable in these circumstances that the conflict between Gandhi and the Working Committee should break out in a more acute form than in the first few days after the outbreak of the war. The majority of the Working Committee felt that here was a situation in which the very immensity of the danger to Britain's own national security may force British statesmen to seek a settlement with the Congress in India. If that happened, then it would obviously be inconvenient for the Congress to be saddled with the leadership of a man who declared that whatever support is to be given to the British should be given on a purely non-violent basis.

After prolonged discussions in which Gandhi participated, the Working Committee announced on 21 June that they were not able to extend the creed on non-violent struggle. The Committee declared in its resolution: 'Mahatma Gandhi desires the Congress to be true to the creed of non-violence and to declare its unwillingness that India should maintain armed forces to defend her freedom against external aggression or internal disorder,' while they themselves 'are unable to go to the full length with

Gandhiji'; but they recognize that he should be 'free to pursue his great ideal in his own way and therefore absolve him from the responsibility for the programme and activity which the Congress has to pursue' (V, p. 355).

This was soon followed by a meeting of the AICC at Poona at which President Azad said:

> The Congress is a political organization, pledged to win the political independence of the country. It is not an institution for organizing world peace. Honestly, we cannot go as far as Mahatma Gandhi wants us to go. We admit that it is a weakness on our part, but it is a weakness which we share with the entire humanity. We have to solve every difficulty that presents itself to us, and we have also to recognize the hard fact of Mahatma Gandhi's separation from the Congress. We must bear it bravely (V, p. 384).

This was the session of the AICC which made the well-known 'Poona Offer'—the offer that the Congress was prepared to participate in a national government in order to defend the country against external aggression, provided, of course, the British government declared its readiness to recognize the freedom of India after the war.

This, however, did not meet with the expected response from the side of the British. The 'Poona Offer' of the Congress in July was countered by the 'August Offer' of the British in which the Viceroy said that the new constitution should be framed by Indians themselves but under two conditions: firstly, the British obligations must be fulfilled and secondly, the minority opinions must not be overrun. It was clear that the British were still continuing the old policy of relying on their four pillars of rule. It is therefore not surprising if the Congress felt, in Tendulkar's words, 'badly let down.' It had openly disagreed with Gandhi, he continues, 'it expressed its inability to extend the principle of non-violence to the national defence of India and had set forth the conditions which would enable it to throw its full weight into the war effort.'

This open rejection of the Congress offer by the British government once again led to the resolution of the conflict between Gandhi and the Working Committee. The Committee called an emergency meeting of the AICC at which President Azad said:

> These events made us decide to again request Mahatma Gandhi to assume the active leadership of the Congress. I am glad to inform you that he has agreed to do this, as now there is no difference whatsoever between him and the Working Committee (V, p. 396).

The resolution drafted by Gandhi was then adopted by the AICC which declared:

This committee firmly believes in the policy and practice of non-violence not only in the struggle for Swaraj but also, in so far as this may be possible of application, in free India (V, p. 397).

It was this resolution of the AICC that led to the anti-war individual satyagraha launched in 1940–41. This satyagraha launched first by Acharaya Vinoba Bhave, then by other individual satyagrahis selected by Gandhi himself, and then by several satyagrahis again selected by Gandhi, continued for several months. This form of satyagraha did not, nor was it meant to, do anything more than registering the protest of the nation against its being drawn into the war efforts of Britain. Gandhi made it clear in several of his speeches and statements that the struggle that was launched was not the struggle for independence, 'that for the time being, we should be satisfied with complete freedom of speech and pen.' He also stated categorically that he did not expect the struggle to end in victory: 'We are resisting an authority that is itself struggling to fight for life against a stubborn foe. . . . Our struggle must be co-terminous at least with the Europeans.'

It is, however, significant that a few months later, in December 1941, the Gandhi-Working Committee conflict did break out once again: Gandhi asked for being relieved of the responsibility laid upon him by the Bombay (September 1940) resolution and the Working Committee agreed to do so. The circumstances under which this happened are described by Tendulkar as follows:

> 1. In mid-June, the international situation suddenly changed when Germany invaded Russia. In July, the expansion of the Viceroy's Executive Council and the formation of a National Defence Council were announced.
> 2. By the late autumn of 1941, it had become obvious that something must be done quickly to improve political situation and enlist the full cooperation of the people in the war. Germany was advancing steadily into Russia and a German drive through the Near-East was expected. Japan had consolidated her position in Indo-China, and was preparing for a final plunge in the war. The mobilization of India's vast resources and manpower had become an urgent military necessity.
>
> On the eve of the Pearl Harbour debacle, the British government made a conciliatory gesture (VI, pp. 14–17). (This conciliatory gesture was the release of the civil disobedience prisoners including Pandit Jawaharlal Nehru and Maulana Abul Kalam Azad.—*E.M.S.N.*)
> 3. On December 23, 1941, the Working Committee met at Bardoli to review the situation as it had developed since its last meeting held fourteen months ago. Japan having plunged in the war, the committee had to take a realistic view of the menacing situation (VI, p, 41).

This 'realistic view of the menacing situation' led Gandhi to write a letter to the Working Committee in which he expressed his surprise at the difference between his interpretation of the Bombay resolution and that of others. He went on to say:

> On re-reading the Bombay resolution I found that the differing members were right and that I had read into it a meaning which its letter could not bear. The discovery of the error makes it impossible for me to lead the Congress in the

> struggle for resistance to the war effort on the grounds in which non-violence was not indispensable . . . . You will, therefore, please relieve me of the responsibility laid upon me by the Bombay resolution (VI, p. 42).

The Working Committee, of course, readily accepted his suggestion and thus once again cleared the path for any negotiations which the government may want to initiate.

> 4. Events were moving with lightning speed. The allies suffered reverses both in Asia and Europe. . . . The debacle of the British forces in Burma was actually felt in China. In February, 1942, Marshal and Madame Chiang Kai-shek visited Delhi and boldly addressed an outspoken appeal to Britain and India. The Marshal appealed to the rulers to grant political power to the Indians (VI, p. 73).
> 5. All these developments forced the British to initiate negotiations.

When Rangoon fell on March 7, 1942, it seemed as if the tide of Japanese conquest would soon be sweeping into Bengal and Madras. On March 11, Churchill announced that the War Cabinet had agreed on a plan for India and that Sir Stafford Cripps had consented to go to India to ascertain whether this plan would secure a 'reasonable and practical' measure of acceptance and 'thus promote the concentration of all Indian thought and energies' on defence against Japan. (VI, p. 87).

'Quit India' and After

The narration of evens in the last chapter makes it clear that the question at issue between the Congress Working Committee and Gandhi was, by no means, the ethics or otherwise of the use of violence in national defence, but one of how to negotiate with, and put pressure on, the British.

Gandhi's advocacy of non-violence pure and simple, his determination to fight the war efforts in a non-violent way, proved effective as a form of pressure against the British. The Working Committee, therefore, always put itself under his leadership whenever there was necessity for giving a threat of struggle or for organizing a struggle.

On the other hand, whenever there was an opportunity for negotiations with the British, the Working Committee took a 'realistic position' that negotiations could be conducted only on the basis of offering India's cooperation with the British if power is transferred. On all such occasions, Gandhi himself asked that he should be relieved of leadership and to which the Working Committee readily agreed. This evidently was an admirable arrangement which perfectly suited the basic strategy of the bourgeoisie: negotiations with the British, supported with mass pressure.

The biggest example of the conflict and agreement between Gandhi and the rest of the Congress leadership was the manner in which subsequent negotiations were conducted between the Congress and the representative of the British.

It was for the specific purpose of enabling the Congress Working Committee to carry on negotiations that Gandhi gave up his leadership of the Congress towards the end of 1941 and in the beginning of 1942. While the negotiations were formally conducted by the Congress president and the Working Committee, Gandhi's advice was nevertheless sought at every stage.

While Gandhi himself kept formally out of the negotiations, his was the voice which was decisive in shaping the policy of the Congress negotiators. Furthermore, the moment the negotiations broke down, the moment it was clear that the British were not prepared to grant the minimum that was demanded of them by the Congress, Gandhi once again came to the forefront as the leader of the anti-war anti-British mass movement. It was he who coined the well-known slogan: 'Quit India.'

One cannot but be struck by the difference between Gandhi's attitude to the British in 1940–41 and his attitude in 1942. The struggle which was launched in 1940–41 under his leadership, Gandhi made it clear, was not a struggle for independence. He asked:

> How are we to fight for independence with those whose own independence is in grave peril? Even if independence can be given by one nation to another, it is not possible for the English. Those who are themselves in peril cannot save others. But, if they fight unto death for their freedom and they are at all reasonable, they must recognize our right of free speech (V, p. 48).

In 1942, however, he was of a different opinion. He said:

> My firm opinion is that the British should leave now in an orderly manner and not run the risk that they did in Singapore, Malaya, and Burma. The act would mean courage of a high order, confession of human limitations and right doing by India (VI, p. 92).

To this contrast in the objectives—between 'freedom of speech and nothing more' and 'independence here and now'—we may well add the contrast in the methods of struggle. In 1940–41, Gandhi restricted the struggle to a few satyagrahis selected by him on the basis of certain severe tests laid down by him. He frowned on all those who made suggestions that the satyagraha should not be restricted to a few selected individuals, but should be made a mass struggle. 'It did not matter' he said, 'how few the satyagrahis might be; if they were only 10 or 12, they would represent the whole of the Congress.' 'Does not one ambassador represent his people?' asked Gandhi.

His attitude in 1942 was entirely different. For the first time in his life, he did not denounce the masses of the people for having resorted to violence. Departing from his traditional outlook on militant mass actions (as at the time of Chauri Chaura, etc.), he now took the stand that whatever 'mob violence' took place was the natural reaction to the 'leonine violence' resorted to by the government.

There are also indications that, in the days before 8 August 1942, Gandhi had visualized that a spontaneous rising of the people would take place when the 'Quit India' struggle was launched. For once in his life, he talked of a mass struggle in which the millions of peasants would rise in revolt not only against the British government but also against landlords. For example, he told the American journalist, Mr. Louis Fischer, that the peasants would begin with non-payment of taxes but that 'refusal to pay it will give the peasants courage to thing that they are capable of independent action. Their next step will be to seize the land.'

> 'With violence?' Mr. Fisher asked.
>
> 'There may be violence,' Gandhi replied, 'but then again, landlords may cooperate.'
>
> 'You are an optimist,' Mr. Fischer remarked.
>
> 'They might cooperate by fleeing,' Gandhi said.
>
> 'Or,' Mr. Fischer said, 'they might organize violent resistance.'
>
> 'There may be fifteen days of chaos,' Gandhi said, 'but I think we would soon bring that under control' (VI, p. 122).

It would, however, be wrong from this to conclude that Gandhi had visualized a real revolutionary struggle of the people. For, though he talked of 'peasants seizing land,' 'fifteen days of chaos,' etc., in the days in which he was popularizing the idea of a struggle to enforce the demand for British withdrawal, he did not make any serious preparations to launch and lead revolutionary actions of the organized working class and the peasantry.

It is significant in this connection that Gandhi's two-hour speech at the AICC session contained not a word addressed to the workers or the peasants: A major part of the speech was devoted to an exposition of his and the Congress' attitude to the Hindu-Muslim question; then a few words on the need for great sacrifice in carrying on the struggle (his slogan 'Do or Die'); following this, special appeals to the journalists, to the princes, to the government servants, to the soldiers and to the students, telling each section as to what they could and should do in support of the 'Quit India' struggle. The overwhelming majority of the people, i.e., the workers and peasants, did not come into Gandhi's picture at all. They had no special role to play—except as a silent mob ready to sacrifice for the slogan of 'Do or Die.'

That this omission was by no means casual will be clear from the 'draft of instructions' which Gandhi had prepared for the Working Committee. The draft calls for a day for *hartal* (similar to the one with which he inaugurated the non-cooperation movement over two decades ago). But he laid down that, 'On the day of the *hartal*, no processions should be taken out, nor meetings held in the cities, all people should observe a twenty-four hours' fast and offer prayers.' No doubt he allowed meetings and processions in villages 'where there is no fear of violence or disturbance.' It was thus clear that, in this struggle as in the earlier ones, one of Gandhi's chief objectives was to prevent militant demonstrations and actions by the mass of the toiling people.

It is also significant that his draft of instructions took abundant precautions against possible outbreak of any anti-landlord action of the peasantry. Going back on the Louis Fischer interview, he asked the peasants to restrict themselves to struggle against the government alone:

> Where the zamindari system prevails, the zamindars pay the

> tax to the government and the ryot to the zamindar. In such cases, if the zamindar makes common cause with the ryot, his portion of the revenue, which may be settled by mutual agreement, should be given to him. But if a zamindar wants to side with the government, no tax should be paid to him (VI, p. 215).

There is, therefore, no cause for the assumption, still made by several political groups and individuals, that the 'August Revolution' had been planned by Gandhi as a really revolutionary mass struggle. It is undoubtedly true that this was the struggle in which Gandhi was far less anxious than any time before to prevent militant mass actions of the people. He had visualized and had actually desired, that the launching of struggle would unleash a lot of mass energy, initiative and militancy. He did not mind very much if these mass actions departed from those strict rules of *ahimsa* which he had insisted upon in earlier struggles. But does it mean that he wanted this struggle to be directed on an uncompromisingly militant mass action, which would end the total defeat of the imperialists and their Indian agents?

Facts unmistakably show that Gandhi had no such ideas. The very fact that he visualized the struggle would end in a few days, that it would be a 'short and swift' struggle, shows that he hoped that the spontaneous actions of the people would force the government to seek for terms. He was obviously hoping that if there was chaos in the country even for a few days, for example, the mass of the people spontaneously expressed their anger and resorted to such militant actions as did paralyze the governmental machinery—if, again, the government servants and soldiers responded to his call 'to obey only those orders of the government that are just,' then a situation would be created in which the leaders of the Allied Powers would put still greater pressure on the British and force them to concede the Indian demand.

It should be noted in this connection that a major part of Gandhi's speeches and writings during the pre-August weeks was addressed to the Allied Powers and their leaders. Through a series of interviews with foreign correspondents, through personal letters addressed to Marshal Chiang kai-shek and President Roosevelt, through repeated references to the necessity for 'defending Russia and China,' through a special appeal 'to the foreign press and through them to the world' and lastly in his speech at the AICC meeting itself—through all this Gandhi made it clear that he expected the Allied Powers to intercede with Britain on India's behalf. Maulana Azad too, in his speech winding up the proceedings of the AICC, 'stated that he was addressing the United Nations on the Congress demand and would strive till the last minute to reach a settlement.'

A few weeks after the Bombay AICC meeting showed that this calculation was wrong. Neither was the mass upsurge strong enough to paralyze the governmental machinery nor were the leaders of the Allied Powers willing to put sufficient pressure on the British government to concede the Indian demand. 'By the end of September,' says Tendulkar, 'the government had apparently succeeded in crushing both the non-violent and the violent attempts to compel them to quit India.'

Just as in 1932, so too now, Gandhi undertook a fast inside jail. Both the 1932 as well as the 1943 fasts were undertaken ostensibly on a non-political, moral issue. But, in the case of both, these non-political moral issues were used as the starting point of a political action—launching of negotiations with the British on political issues.

We have seen in an earlier chapter how the ostensibly social question of the place of Harijans in Hindu society was taken up by Gandhi in 1932 for a fast inside jail—with a view to having the British Prime Minister's Communal Award modified—which itself was to have been, in its turn, used for negotiations on the constitutional issue. So too in 1942–43, Gandhi took up allegations made by the government in justification of its repressive policies following the August meeting of the AICC, and made it an ostensibly moral issue. However, this was by no means a moral issue, but a political one, as can be seen from the following summary of his stand which he gave in a letter to the Viceroy, dated January 1943:

> To sum up: (1) If you want me to act singly, convince me that I was wrong and I will make ample amends. (2) If you want me to make a proposal on behalf of the Congress, you should put me among the Working Committee members. I plead that you make up your mind to end the impasse (VI, pp. 234–35).

The government, however, was not prepared to accept Gandhi's suggestions. This provoked him to go on a fast, which particularly at his age, raised alarm and panic throughout the country. To this sense of general anxiety for his life, the government had to respond; it allowed several visitors to see him during the fast. This was the beginning of a campaign for the release of the Congress leaders and for the opening of negotiations between the Congress and the government.

Gandhi made it clear to his visitors that he would do his best to solve the political impasse which followed the Quit India movement and the subsequent arrest of Congress leaders. The non-Congress leaders, who met in Bombay in March, issued a statement, in which they said:

> The recent talks which some of us have had with Gandhi lead us to believe that a move for reconciliation at the present juncture will bear fruit. It is our conviction that, if Gandhi is set at liberty, he will do his best to give guidance and assistance in the solution of internal deadlock and that there need be no fear that there would be any danger for the successful prosecution of war (VI, p. 250)

Just as on the question of negotiations between the government and the Congress, so on the question of negotiations between the Congress and Muslim League, Gandhi had changed from the stand which he had taken during the days of the Quit India movement. This was made clear by Rajagopalachari more than a year later:

> On 10 July 1944, Rajagopalachari published the formula which had been discussed with and had been approved by Gandhi during his fast in 1943. The formula was intended to serve as a basis for a settlement between the Congress and the Muslim League. (VI, p. 332).

Gandhi also made attempts to establish direct contact with Jinnah. Referring to Jinnah's complaint as to 'Why does he (Gandhi) not write to me direct?' Gandhi wrote in the beginning of May:

> I welcome your invitation. I suggest our meeting face to face rather than our talking through correspondence. . . . Why should not you and I approach the great question of communal unity as men determined on finding a common solution and work together to make our solution acceptable to all who are concerned with it or are interested in it? (VI, pp. 259–60).

The government, however, refused to respond either on the question of negotiations between the government and the Congress or on the question of facilitating negotiations between the Congress and the Muslim League. In their replies to Gandhi's letters preceding his fast, they took the stand that Gandhi should dissociate himself from the August resolution of the AICC and condemn the acts of violence on the part of the people and of several Congress leaders. The request of the non-Congress leaders for permission to see Gandhi was turned down by the government on the following ground:

> So long as the Congress policy remains what it is, there can be no question of any alteration in our attitude towards the

> Congress. . . . With every respect for your good intentions and your anxiety to see a happy solution, I cannot agree to give special facilities such as you ask for contact with Mr. Gandhi and other leaders, while conditions remain as I have described them (VI, pp. 251–52).

As for Gandhi's letter to Jinnah, the government simply refused to forward it to him on the ground that

> they (government) are not prepared to give facilities for political correspondence or contact to a person detained for promoting an illegal mass movement which he had not disavowed and thus gravely embarrassing India's war effort at a critical time (VI, p. 260).

The political impasse, therefore, continued for the whole of 1943 and the first half of 1944. The nation was angry and indignant over the continued detention of the Congress leaders, but the government was not prepared to accede to the demand for their release. It was only in May 1944, and that too, when his health deteriorated considerably, that Gandhi was released.

This release, however, made a slight change in the situation, since it made it possible for Gandhi to publicly put his weight in favour of a new policy both on the question of Congress-government relations, as well as on the Hindu-Muslim question. He took a series of steps which were calculated to facilitate a reconsideration of the policy by all the parties concerned.

First of all, he took the opportunity of a press interview with Mr. Stewart Gelder, the correspondent of *News Chronicle*, to express his views on the political situation of the time. In the course of this interview, he was reported to have stated

> that there was a difference between what he would ask today and what was asked in 1942. Today, he would be satisfied with a national government in full control of civil administration. It was not so in 1942 (VI, p. 318).

This was not an ordinary press interview. It 'constituted my (Gandhi's) individual effort to end the present deadlock. They are more addressed to the powers that be than to the people.' He also addressed two letters to the Viceroy following the Gelder interview, in the course of which he made the following categorical statement:

> I am prepared to advise the Working Committee to declare that, in view of the changed conditions, mass civil disobedience, envisaged by the resolution of August 1942, cannot be offered and that full cooperation in the war effort should be given by the Congress, if a declaration of immediate Indian independence is made and a national government responsible to the central assembly be formed subject to the proviso that during the pendency of war, the military operations should continue as at present, but without involving any financial burden on India. If there is a desire on the part of the British government for a settlement, friendly talks should take the place of correspondence. But I am in your hands (VI, pp. 327–28).

Secondly, together with these negotiations with the government, Gandhi also started negotiations with the Muslim League. The well-known Gandhi-Jinnah talks started in September on the basis of the Rajagopalachari formula which, as a matter of fact, was a new version of the proposals which Rajagopalachari had made in 1942 and which had been rejected at the time by an overwhelming majority of the Congress

Thirdly and finally, Gandhi clarified his stand on the question of the August struggle. 'The government went mad, and so did some people. Sabotage and the like were resorted to and many things were done in the Congress name or in my name.' On the question of observing 9th August in 1944, he advised the people 'not to disregard special police prohibitions for that day' except in Bombay. Even in Bombay, a place 'most easily accessible to me and the place where the historic meeting of August '42 was held,' the defiance of police prohibition was to be symbolic. He also directed 'those who have gone underground to discover themselves. They can do so by informing the authorities of their work in the open without any attempt to evade or elude the police.' Here, therefore, was a programme of prohibiting any defiance of authority on a countrywide scale, but of symbolically holding the banner of resistance aloft.

It was at the very time when Gandhi was making these efforts at negotiations that Subhas Bose was organizing the Indian National Army. The two policies pursued by the two leaders were mutually contradictory: one was an attempt to retreat from the Quit India movement; the other was trying to carry the movement forward by bringing armed forces from outside to help the forces of revolt within the country.

Yet, the two were in a sense supplementing each other. Though Gandhi was seeking a way of retreat, he was holding the banner of resistance aloft, as was clear from his 'symbolic defiance' instruction in Bombay on 9th August. That is why we find, on the occasion of Gandhi's 75th birthday in October 1944, Netaji declaring in a speech in Rangoon: 'Father of Our Nation! In this holy war for India's liberation, we ask for your blessings and good wishes.' Gandhi, for his part, refrained from making any comment, favourable or unfavourable, on Netaji's programme and activities.

Both polices, however, failed in their immediate objective. Gandhi's efforts at negotiations broke against the impenetrable wall of obstruction put up by the British government. His offer of full cooperation in the war effort provided Indian independence was immediately declared and a national government formed, evoked the reply from the viceroy that 'it is impossible during the period of hostilities to bring about any change in the constitution by which means alone a national government such as you suggest can be made responsible to the central assembly.' His negotiations with the Muslim League too ended in failure, because Jinnah rejected the Rajaji formula and also the terms suggested by Gandhi which, according to him, were 'calculated to completely torpedo the Pakistan demand of Muslim India.'

While Gandhi's policy of seeking ways of retreat from the August 1942 position had thus temporarily proved a failure, so too did Netaji's policy. The opening of the second front in Europe in 194, the rapid advance of the Soviet Red Army into Germany and the heroic struggle of the resistance fighters in China and other Asian countries were making it clear that Netaji's policy of an internal revolutionary movement, assisted from abroad by armed forces organized in cooperation with the Japanese fascists, had proved abortive. In a few months after its formation, the Indian National Army and its Japanese allies had to meet the reformed and reorganized forces of the Allied camp at whose hands they suffered defeat in the end. The INA disappeared from the scene except as a force which, because of its very nature and objective, evoked pride and patriotism in the Indian people.

These very international developments, however, had their impact on the internal political situation. The inexorable advance of the Allied forces made it impossible for the British government to continue to keep the Congress leaders in detention, or to maintain the stand that no question of constitutional changes arose because of the conditions of war. It had become necessary for the government to take new steps in the direction of making fresh efforts at solving the internal political crisis.

These new efforts started with the release of the members of the Congress Working Committee in the release of the members of the Congress Working Committee in the middle of June, 1945. This was followed by certain proposals for the re-constitution of the central executive council,

> so that all its members except the governor-general and the commander-in-chief, would be the Indian political leaders, the caste Hindu and the Muslims being equally represented. . . . In furtherance of this plan, the viceroy will call a conference of the party leaders and provincial premiers and ex-premiers, who will be asked to submit to him lists of names, from which he can select the personnel of the new executive council (VII, p. 7).

These efforts, however, failed because of Jinnah's objection to the inclusion of two nationalist Muslims, Maulana Azad and Asaf Ali, in the council of ministers. It was becoming clearer that the communal question in general and the Hindu-Muslim question in particular, was being taken advantage of by the British rulers to prevent any change of government.

This raised a storm of indignation among the mass of the people, who were coming to see in clearer and sharper terms the real nature of the policies of the government. The failure of the negotiations for the formation of a national government was followed by the great countrywide campaign for the release of the INA prisoners. The defence of the INA prisoners, who were being tried in the latter half of 1945, became the focal point of a new wave of anti-imperialist struggles. As Tendulkar says:

> Nehru was present in the court in his barrister's robes, which he had discarded thirty years ago. Bhulabhai Desai, the defence counsel, concentrated the nation's attention on the great role played by the Indian National Army under the inspiring leadership of Subhas Chandra Bose. . . . The country demanded the freedom of the INA accused and ultimately secured it. 'It became a trial of strength' said Nehru, 'between the will of the Indian people and the will of those who hold power in India and it was the will of the people that triumphed in the end' (VII, pp. 17–8).

While the cause of the men of the Indian National Army was thus galvanizing the anti-imperialist movement, that very movement was having its impact on the men of the Indian armed forces under the British. The revolt of the Royal Indian Navy symbolized the fact that neither the crushing of the 1942 struggle nor the defeat of the INA had dampened the spirit of Indian resistance.

Gandhi became extremely perturbed over the whole situation. A week before the RIN mutiny, he had written in *Harijan*:

> Hatred is in the air and the impatient lovers of the country will gladly take advantage of it, if they can, through violence, to further the cause of independence. . . . The hypnotism of the INA has cast its spell upon us. Netaji's name is one to conjure with. His patriotism is second to none. . . . My praise and my admiration can go no further. For I knew that his action was doomed to failure, and that I would have said so, even if he had brought his INA victorious to India, because the masses would not have come into their own in this manner (VII, pp. 76–8).

On the RIN mutiny, he said that he had followed the events 'with painful interest.' He went on:

> This mutiny in the navy and what is following is not, in any sense of the term, non-violent action. . . If the Indian members of the navy know and appreciate non-violence, the way of non-violent resistance can be dignified, manly and wholly effective, if it is corporate. . . . Action like this, I have called non-violent non-cooperation. As it is, they are setting a bad and unbecoming example for India (VII, pp. 78–9).

This new wave of the anti-imperialist movement made it obvious to the British government that they could not rule in the old way. They therefore decided to take new steps to settle the political crisis. A delegation of three cabinet ministers was sent to India to carry on negotiations with the various Indian parties.

They conducted protracted negotiations in April and May and came out with long-term and short-term proposals. The long-term proposals envisaged the setting up of a constituent assembly elected by the newly elected provincial legislatures. The provinces were to be grouped into A, B, and C and each of the groups were given the right to secede from the Union—an arrangement which would partially meet the demand of the Muslim League. The short-term proposals related to the formation of an interim government consisting of representatives of the Congress, the Muslim League and other parties and groups.

It was these proposals which, after protracted negotiations, led to the formation of the interim government in the latter half of 1946, and a year later, to the creation of the two independent States of India and Pakistan.

August 15: Triumph or Defeat?

The transfer of power in 1947 is paraded by the Congress leader as a unique event in world history. They claim that, unlike other revolutions in the world, such as the French, the Russian, the Chinese, etc., the Indian revolution of 1947 was brought about without shedding a drop of blood, since it was led by the apostle of non-violence.

This is a claim which was officially made on 15 August 1957. The 'message to the nation' issued by the then Congress President, Acharya Kripalani, claimed:

> Never before was so great an event transforming the destiny of millions of men and women consummated with such little bloodshed and violence. . . . that this has been possible is due to the inspiring leadership of Mahatma Gandhi, who, if any man may be so-called, is the Father of our Nation. He has led us in the non-violent battle for freedom and he has shown us the way to make this freedom fruitful in the service of our people (VIII, p. 95).

One man, however, did not share this view. That man was Mahatma Gandhi himself. Tendulkar states:

> There were festivities all over the land. But the man who, more than any one else, had been responsible for freeing India from the alien rule did not participate in these rejoicings. When an officer of the Information and Broadcasting Department of the Government of India came for a message, Gandhi replied that 'he had run dry.' When told again that if he did not give any message, it would not be good, Gandhi replied: 'There is no message at all, if it is bad, let it be so.' (VIII, pp. 95–6).

More than five months later, on 26 January 1948—just four days before he was murdered—he observed:

> This day, 26th January, is Independence Day. This observance was quite appropriate, when we were fighting for independence we had not seen, nor handled. Now! We have handled it and we seem to be disillusioned. At least I am, even if you are not (VIII, p. 338).

The main reason for this disillusionment was the wave of communal frenzy that was spreading throughout the country, in the wake of the 1946–47 negotiations between the representatives of the British government and the leaders of the Indian National Congress, Muslim League and other parties. Never was such a frenzy witnessed in the history of India's national movement; never were so many Muslims on the one hand and Hindus and Sikhs on the other, cold-bloodedly murdered by one another as in those months preceding and following 15 August.

It had always been Gandhi's claim that the path which he had charted out for the Indian people was the path of love, rather than of hatred. If only the Indian people chose this path, they would be able to bring about a change in the heart of even the most violent and brutal oppressors of the nation—the British imperialists. Yet, here was a situation in which his method failed even in uniting the hearts of our own Indian people, not to speak of changing the hearts of British imperialists.

It should be said to Gandhi's credit that he was perhaps the only leader of the Congress who 'frankly and fully' admitted that the developments leading up to the transfer of power were indicative not of the triumph but of the defeat of the principles which he had been preaching during his whole lifetime. He said on 14 July:

> What we had practised during the past thirty years was not non-violent resistance, but passive resistance, which only the weak offer because they are unable, not unwilling, to offer an

> armed resistance. If we knew the use of non-violent resistance, which only those with the hearts of oak can offer, we would present to the world a totally different picture of free India, instead of an India cut in twain, one part highly suspicious of the other and the two too much engaged in mutual strife to be able to think cogently of the food and clothing of the hungry and naked millions, who know no religion but that of the one and only God, who appears to them in the guise of necessaries of life (VII, p. 57).

It should further be said to Gandhi's credit that he continued up to the last moment of his life and to the last ounce of his energy to fight against the evil forces of communalism according to his light. From the first moment when signs were available of the dangerous communal frenzy that was spreading throughout the country—ever since the outbreak of the first communal riot in Calcutta on 16 August 1946, which had been declared by the Muslim League as 'Direct Action Day'—he devoted himself to the task of preaching communal harmony. When the riots started spreading from cities to the villages, he gave up all other activities in order to spread his message of unity. It was to this end that he spent several weeks in the Noakhali district of Bengal, going from village to village. It was again for this that he left Noakhali for Bihar, wanted to go to the Punjab, went to Calcutta, and to Delhi. Fighting the communal frenzy, defending the victims of riots, giving succour to refugees, etc., became the main theme of his daily post-prayer addresses.

It was, however, becoming clear that the message that he was preaching was becoming less effective than ever before. There had been occasions in the past when his very presence, or at best his undertaking a fast, was effective in bringing the people of different communities together, in preventing the accentuation of the communal situation. Now too, his presence first in Noakhali, then in Bihar, Calcutta, Delhi and other places helped the cause of preventing riots to a certain extent or for a time; but not even the concentration of all his energies to this particular cause was sufficient to bring about any appreciable change in the situation even in the locality where he worked, not to speak of distant places.

The situation was so serious that, at one moment, Gandhi even drew the attention of the people to the possibility of a war between the two states of India and Pakistan. This naturally produced a great sensation in the country, some people even suggesting that such a war would have Gandhi's approval. He was, therefore, compelled to explain the circumstances in which he had to refer to the possibility of war:

> We have among us the superstition that the mere mention of a snake ensures its appearance in the house in which the mention is made even by a child. I hope that no one in India entertains such superstition about war. I claim that I rendered a service to both the sister states by examining the present situation, and definitely stating when the cause of war could arise between the two States. And this was done not to promote war, but to avoid it as far as possible. I endeavoured, too, to show that if the insensate murders, loot and arson by the people continued, they would force the hands of their governments. Was it wrong to draw public attention to the logical steps, that inevitably followed one after another? (VIII, pp. 169–70).

Gandhi also knew that the relations between the two communities were so strained that any one who attempted to bring about communal unity would earn the hatred of fanatics on both sides. He knew that he himself was taking great personal risks in fighting the communal frenzy. Recall his reference in the course of a talk with Rajkumari Amrit Kaur on 28 January, to the possibility of his 'dying by the bullets of a mad man' and his promise that, if it happens, he would 'do so smiling. There must be no anger within me. God must be in my heart and on my lips,' he said. These words have a melancholy ring today in the light of what happened just two days later.

Though these were the distressing developments that

prevented Gandhi from joining the festivities of 15 August, no less important were the developments inside the Congress itself. For some time even before the transfer of power, Gandhi had been worried to see Congressmen trying to promote their personal ends through the organization of which they were members. For example, he wrote in July 1946 in a note entitled 'A Tragic Phenomenon':

> My post contains so many letters from persons who want to be in the constituent assembly, that it frightens me into the suspicion that, if these letters are an indication of the general feeling, the intelligentsia is more anxious about personal aggrandizement than about India's independence. . . . I write this more to draw attention to the disease, of which these applications are a sign, than to warn my correspondents against building any expectation of my intervention (VII, p. 186).

The 'disease', however, developed further and became a very serious problem to which Gandhi's attention was drawn by several of his correspondents. It was this, along with the dangerous communal situation, that impelled Gandhi to undertake his last fast in January 1948. In the course of his prayer speech on the evening of 12 January, at which he announced his decision to fast from the 13th, he quoted from a letter which he had received from the veteran Andhra Congressman, Deshbhakta Konda Venkatappayya. That letter stated:

> The one great problem apart from many other political and economic issues of a very complicated nature, is the moral degradation into which the men in the Congress circles have fallen. I cannot say much about other provinces, but in my province, conditions are very deplorable. The taste of political power has turned their heads. . . . The factions in the Congress circles, the money-making activities of several of the MLAs and MLCs, and the weakness of the ministers

> have been creating a rebellious spirit amongst the people at large. The people have begun to say that the British government was much better and they are even cursing the Congress (VIII, pp. 302–03).

While factional squabbles and power politics were thus rampant in the provincial and district Congress committees, they were not totally absent in the central leadership either. A minor crisis broke out in the all-India leadership in November, 1947.

> On the very first day in the presence of Gandhi, president Kripalani told the AICC, that he was resigning his position. He had neither been consulted by the government, nor had been taken into their full confidence. He said that the government ignored the Congress party. Gandhi, Kripalani revealed, felt that, in these circumstances, the resignation was justified. Nehru and Patel were the heads of the government. Their popularity and hold on the Congress machine was unquestioned. They identified themselves with the party. Why then should they accept the Congress president as a curb on their power? (VIII, p. 233).

While this crisis was tided over by the acceptance of Kripalani's resignations and his replacement by Rajendra Prasad, the relations between Sardar Patel and Jawaharlal Nehru deteriorated further. Tendulkar observes that 'Gandhi knew of the friction between Sardar and Nehru and it worried him. He wanted them to hold together.' It was in this connection that he had a meeting with Sardar Patel at 4 p.m., on January 30—an hour before he was murdered. It was in this connection, again, that 'Nehru and Azad were to see him after the evening prayers.'

These internal developments in the Congress made Gandhi give serious thought to the future of the Congress. In the well-known draft constitution for a reorganized Congress, prepared by him in his last days, he stated:

> The Congress, in its present shape and form, as a propaganda vehicle and a parliamentary machine, has outlived its use. India has still to attain social, moral and economic independence in terms of India's seven hundred thousand villages, as distinguished from its cities and towns. The struggle for the ascendancy of civil over military power is bound to take place in India's progress towards its democratic goal. The Congress must be kept out of unhealthy competition with the political parties and communal bodies. For these and other similar reasons, the All India Congress Committee resolves to disband the existing Congress organization and flower into a Lok Sewak Sangh under the following rules with the power to alter them as occasion may demand (VIII, p. 342).

It is characteristic of Gandhi, that while all his lieutenants were celebrating the attainment of complete independence, he was more concerned with the instability of the newly-created Indian state than feeling happy at its formation. While the other leaders of the Congress were acclaiming the transfer of power as the triumph of the Indian national movement under their leadership, he made it his job to draw people's attention to the two main sources of India's political instability: *firstly*, the strained relations between Hindus and Muslims, which, in its turn, led to strained relations between the two newly-created States of India and Pakistan; and *secondly*, the decay and degradation inside the Congress organization.

It is this that marks him out from the other leaders of the Congress. With his finger on the pulse of the people, Gandhi was able to see that, unless a radical transformation was brought about in the state of Hindu-Muslim relations and unless the state of internal organization of the Congress was improved, the new Indian state was in danger of collapse.

Furthermore, Gandhi had no personal axe to grind, he represented the bourgeois class as a whole and not an individual or group among the bourgeoisie; he was therefore able to look at every problem from the point of view of the long-range interests of his class as a whole, rather than from the narrow, petty, personal or group interests of sections of the bourgeoisie. He was able to see not only the main sources of the instability of the new state with a certain amount of objectivity, but also to do his utmost to remove these sources of instability. Herein lies the greatness of Gandhi as the ideological-political leader of the Indian bourgeoisie.

Gandhi was able to put his finger at the two main sources of the instability and to see why these sources should arise at the very time when the state was being founded. Characteristically he was, however, unable to give any rational explanation as to why, after three decades of his preaching the gospel of love, he had had the misfortune to see in his last days the Indian people so divided into two warring communal camps that the very consummation of his political aim—the creation of an independent Indian state—led to the creation of two antagonistic States set up on the basis of religion. Nor could he offer any convincing explanation as to why the very people, who had, under his leadership, made tremendous sacrifices for the cause of the nation, started quarrelling among themselves for power and personal aggrandizement.

The only reason which he could find for these distressing developments was that Man—the very Man whose moral regeneration was the objective for which he had evolved his theory and practice of non-violent resistance—had gone mad. But how was it that the three decades in which he preached the gospel of love and non-violence witnessed the transformation not of Man the Mad into Man the Sober, but the other way round? This is a question which so baffled him that he could do nothing more than put his trust in God.

Though he was, in practice, putting up a courageous fight against the evil forces of communalism, he had lost all his self-confidence, lost even his joy of life and will to live. In his reply to a correspondent on the occasion of his birthday in 1947, he wrote:

> Without doubt, the ideal thing would be, neither to wish to

> live 125 years, nor to wish to die now. Mine must be a state of complete resignation to the Divine Will. And if I had the impertinence openly to declare my wish to live 125 years, I must have the humility, under changed circumstances, openly to shed that wish. . . . I invoke the aid of the all-embracing Power to take me away from this 'vale of tears,' rather than make me a helpless witness of the butchery by man become savage, whether he dares to call himself a Muslim or Hindu or what not. (VII, p. 176).

Herein lies the limitation of the greatness of Gandhi. Circumscribed as his vision was by the world-outlook of the bourgeoisie, he was unable to see that neither the deterioration in communal relations nor the degeneration of the Congress on the eve and after the transfer of power was accidental, but the result of the operation of certain laws of social development. If he had been able to see this, he would have known that the Hindu-Muslim conflicts were the results not of something inherently wrong with the mass of Hindus and Muslims but because certain definite social forces were working to incite them against each other. he would then have made up his mind not to leave the fate of the Hindu and Muslim masses to God's will, but would have fought those social forces which were working to bring about Hindu-Muslim conflicts.

Having no such understanding of the social forces working for communal disruption, Gandhi was probably more afraid of unity in the struggle against reactionary elements than even communal riots. Take, for example, how he dreaded the militant unity of Hindus and Muslims which manifested itself in the RIN revolt:

> This mutiny in the navy and what is following is not, in any sense of the term, non-violent action. . . . *A combination between the Hindus and the Muslims and others for the purpose of violent action is unholy and it will lead to and probably is a preparation for mutual violence—bad for India and the world.* . . . Aruna would 'rather unite Hindus and Muslims at the barricade than on the constitution front.' Even in terms of

> violence, this is a misleading proposition. . . . Emphatically it betrays want of foresight to disbelieve the British declarations and precipitate a quarrel in anticipation. . . . Aruna and her comrades have to ask themselves every time whether the non-violent way has or has not raised India from her slumber of ages and has created in them a yearning, very vague perhaps, for Swaraj. There is, in my opinion, only one answer (VII, pp. 78–81. Emphasis added).

The same thing holds true of Gandhi's failure to see the reason for the degeneration of Congressmen. Frowning as he did on the theory of class struggle, acknowledging as he claimed to do the goodness of the individual, even of the landlord and capitalist classes, he was unable to see that the upper and middle class politicians, who composed the leadership of the Congress, were as much likely to quarrel among themselves for personal ends after securing power as they were in making personal sacrifices while fighting for power. Unable to see this reason for the paradoxical phenomenon of hitherto selfless men and women being transformed into shameless self-seekers, Gandhi was unable to offer any explanation for the moral degradation in the ranks of the Congress which he was able to see but not check. The result was that he who began with the assumption of the essential goodness of individuals ended up by the theory of men having run mad and deteriorated.

It is a significant fact of history that the very occasion which gladdened the hearts of millions upon millions of the Indian people—the occasion of their attainment of freedom—was chosen by Gandhi to express the view that his mission in life (regeneration of Man) was a failure. No better, no more convincing verdict can be given of the triumph of Gandhism as the political strategy and tactics of the bourgeoisie in its struggle against the British and its total failure as a new social philosophy, a new method to regenerate Man.

Meaning of Gandhism

What is the significance of the life and teaching of Mahatma Gandhi? Is the story of his life 'the story of his experiments with truth' as he himself put it in the 1920s when he started writing his autobiography?

How are we to explain the evolution of Mohandas Gandhi into the 'Father of the Nation'; the devoted sergeant during the First World War into the leader of the 'Do or Die' movement of 1942, with its inspiring slogan of 'British Rulers, Quit India'; the scion of a family of loyal servants of the feudal rulers of Porbunder State into a fighter for democracy in the Indian States; the religious-minded youth who was not attracted by any of the radical movements, but landed himself in the Society of Vegetarians in London, into the most outstanding leader of the anti-imperialist and democratic movement in out country?

Such are the questions which naturally come to our minds as we close the story of the eventful life briefly outlined in the preceding pages. These are not abstract questions, but questions which have their bearing on the practical tasks which every democrat in our country has to fulfill today. For, though the Mahatma is no more in our midst, his life-long teachings are guiding the activities of several groups and individuals inside the democratic movement.

The Bhoodan movement, for example, is undoubtedly based on Gandhi's teachings; it is a movement with whose theories and practice one may disagree, but which one can never ignore. The two aspects of the Bhoodan movement—its revolt against the existing system of landed property, as well as its insistence that the maldistribution of landed property should be rectified in a 'non-violent' way—are both the application of Gandhi's teachings to the most important social problem of our country, the problem of land distribution.

Let us not forget either that it is because of the inspiration drawn from Gandhi's teachings that several of the present-day Gandhians (including Vinobaji himself) have, in some way or other, associated themselves with the peace movement.

On the other hand, let us not forget that it is in the name of Gandhi's teachings against what is called 'mob violence' that the present-day leaders of the government, both at the Centre and in the States, attack the growing mass movement of the working class and peasantry.

It is a measure of the enormous significance of the role played by Gandhi in the history of our national movement that every trend and faction inside the Congress, and almost every political party barring the Communist Party, uses the name of Gandhi and his teachings for justifying and defending its policies. Serious attempts to assess the role and significance of Gandhi and his teachings should, therefore, be considered of enormous practical importance for the further development of the democratic movement.

This is not an easy task. Like several other historical personages, Gandhi had a highly complex personality; his teachings, too, are incapable of over-simplified assessments on the lines of his being 'the inspirer of the national movement who roused the masses to anti-imperialist action'; 'the counter-revolutionary who did all he could to prevent the development of our national movement on revolutionary lines,' etc.

His life was so rich in events, his speeches and writings so prolific and touched such varied fields of human activity, his actions at various stages so dramatic, that it will be easy enough for any student of his life and teachings to prove his or her own pet theory about Gandhi and Gandhism. What he or she has to do is only to string together a series of selected incidents from his life and selected pronouncements from his speeches and writings. It is, however, far more difficult to select those that are really significant from the point of view of history, see the interconnection between the various aspects of his life and teachings, and then to arrive at an integrated understanding of the man and his mission.

Unfortunately for us, the efforts which have so far been made belong to the two categories—either over-simplified and one-sided tributes, or equally over-simplified and one-sided criticisms. Every effort should, therefore, be made to avoid both these pitfalls. It is as a contribution to such efforts that the conclusions which appear to the present writer to flow from his life are given below.

The *first* point to be noted is that Gandhi was an idealist—idealist not only in the sense that the world-outlook which guided him was opposed to philosophical materialism, but also in the sense that he kept before him certain ideals to which he clung till the end of his life. Moral values like truth, non-violence, renunciation of the pleasures of life, etc.; social objectives such as abolition of caste distinctions, emancipation of women, unity of all religious groups and communities, etc.—these were indivisible parts of his life and teachings. It is this adherence to certain ideals that made him plunge into the South African satyagraha movement in the early part of his public life; it was this again that enabled him to work out his non-cooperation and other campaigns for the freedom of the nation; it was this that made him the champion of innumerable democratic causes and ultimately made him a martyr in the noble cause of national unity.

Secondly, his idealism played a big role in rousing the hitherto slumbering millions of the rural poor. The semi-religious language which he used in speaking to them, the simple unostentatious life which he led, and the passion with which he fought for their demands—all these drew the millions of the rural poor towards him. They looked upon him as their saviour, as a new incarnation of God, out to deliver them from the miserable plight in which they are placed.

We may well consider his views on several social, economic and cultural questions as 'reactionary' (many of them undoubtedly are reactionary). It would, however, be a profound mistake to miss the fact that it was these 'reactionary' views of his that enabled him to form a bridge between the mass of peasantry and the sophisticated representatives and leaders of the modern national-democratic movement. It may appear self-contradictory if one were to say that Gandhi with his 'reactionary' social outlook was instrumental in bringing about a profoundly revolutionary phenomenon—the drawing of the mass of the rural poor into the arena of the modern national-democratic movement. This self-contradiction, however, is a manifestation of the contradiction in the real political life of our nation, arising out of the fact that the national-democratic movement was led by the bourgeoisie, linked with feudalism.

Thirdly, it should be pointed out that, though he played a vital role in drawing the mass of the rural poor into the national movement, it would be wrong to ascribe to him personally the tremendous awakening which they showed in the years after the First World War. For, this awakening was the result of historic developments that were taking place in India as well as throughout the world. The slow and steady deterioration in the economic conditions of the Indian peasantry which reached alarming proportions during and immediately after the First World War; the growth of a radical wing inside the Indian national movement, which in certain areas touched sections of the peasantry as well; the impact of such international developments as the Turkish, Chinese and, above all, Russian revolutions on the minds of the Asian people as a whole—these were some of the basic causes which had started acting on the consciousness of the Indian peasantry. They would have acted—probably not in the same way—even if Gandhi had not come on the scene.

Stating this is not to deny Gandhi's role as an individual in giving a specific character to the awakening of the Indian peasantry, to the fact that the new upsurge came to be linked with the political movement for freedom and democracy. To deny Gandhi's contribution to the drawing of the rural poor and to the consequent strengthening of the national-democratic movement would be as one-sided as to ascribe to him all the credit for the people's awakening itself.

Fourthly, while Gandhi thus deserves praise for his role in overcoming the major weaknesses of the national-democratic movement—making the movement really national and all-class by bringing in the large masses of the hitherto unorganized rural poor—it should not be forgotten that he had always been and continued till his death to be afraid of the rural poor acting as an independent force. While he was all for mobilizing them in the struggle for freedom and democracy, he was keen that they should act under the leadership of his own class, the bourgeoisie.

Ever since the days of Chauri-Chaura, he had taken special care to devise all manner of measures to see that at every stage in the struggle for freedom and democracy, the rural poor kept themselves within the limits which were considered safe for the bourgeoisie. Anybody who fails to recognize this reality will be unable to explain why he was so insistent on non-violence being observed by the people in their struggle against imperialism and their agents, while he had no qualms of conscience in acting as the recruiting sergeant for imperialism during the First World War.

Fifthly, not only in relation to the rural poor, but also in relation to the working class and other sections of the working people, his was an approach which, in actual practice, helped the bourgeoisie. His theory of trusteeship, his insistence on certain moral values as the guiding lines for any political activity, the skilful way in which he combined his own extra-parliamentary activities (constructive programme and satyagraha) with the parliamentary activities of his lieutenants, the characteristically Gandhian way of combining negotiations with the enemy even while carrying on mass direct action against him—all these proved in actual practice to be of enormous help to the bourgeoisie in (*a*) rousing the masses in action against imperialism and in (*b*) preventing them from resorting to revolutionary mass action. This ability of his to rouse the masses and yet to check them, to launch anti-imperialist direct action and yet to go on negotiating with the imperialist rulers made him the undisputed leader of the bourgeoisie. He was a leader in whom all factions and groups inside the class had confidence and who, therefore, could unify and activate it.

Finally, Gandhi's role in history as the foremost leader of the bourgeoisie should not be taken to mean that he was always, and on every issue, at one with the bourgeoisie. On the other hand, it is characteristic of him, and the class of which he was the friend, philosopher and guide, that, on several occasions and on several issues, his was a minority voice, if not a lone voice. On all such occasions, he and they agreed among themselves that they would temporarily go along different paths. This is a phenomenon which manifested itself again and again—first in the post-non-cooperation years (division of labour between Swarajists and no-changers); then in the years after the 1932–33 civil disobedience movement; several times during the Second World War and, finally, in the months preceding and following the attainment of independence.

Particularly was this true of the last days of his life when his idealism came into conflict with the 'iron practicalism' of the 'steel-minded' Sardar Patel, with the modernism of the radical intellectual Pandit Nehru, and several others who had been his colleagues and lieutenants for several years. It was this growing gulf between him and his colleagues that made his life tragic in the post-independence months, even before that life came to a tragic end.

It is when we examine this growing gulf between him and his colleagues in the last days of his life that we come to a really objective all-sided assessment of Gandhi, the man and his mission. For, this growing gulf was the manifestation of the reality that Gandhi's insistence on certain moral values had once been helpful to the bourgeoisie, but became, in the last days of his life, a hindrance.

In the days in which it had to fight on two fronts—fight imperialism and, to this end, bring the mass of our urban and rural poor into action; at the same time, fight the trend towards revolutionary action which was growing among the masses—the bourgeoisie found it quite useful to resort to the technique of non-violent resistance evolved by Gandhi. However, once the struggle against imperialism was crowned with success, in the sense that the bourgeoisie and its class allies got state power, it was no more necessary to fight a two-front battle. Whatever further struggles have to be waged against imperialism can be waged at the state level, for which it was not necessary to draw the masses of our people into action.

Furthermore, the very fact that the bourgeoisie got state power in its hands and had to use it in its own class interests, brought it and its state machinery into ever more conflicts with the mass of our people. Another result of their coming to power was that the individual representatives of the bourgeoisie who came to power (ministers, MPs, and MLAs, etc.) began to enrich themselves and their friends, relatives, hangers-on, etc., at the cost of the state as well as of the people; to this end, they resorted to any and every corrupt method provided they yielded results.

It was this change in the position of the bourgeoisie as a class and its individual representatives that brought it into conflict with Gandhi, the man who still clung to the ideals which he had been preaching in the days of anti-imperialist struggle. The moral values which he had preached in the days of anti-imperialist struggle now became a hindrance to the politicians who came to power. Gandhi, on the other hand, remained true to them and could not reconcile himself to the sudden change which occurred in his former colleagues and lieutenants. Particularly was this so on the question of Hindu-Muslim unity and on the corruption in the ranks of the Congress (both of which have already been described in the preceding chapter).

We may conclude by saying that Gandhi became the Father of the Nation, precisely because the idealism to which he adhered in the years of anti-imperialist struggle became a practically useful political weapon in the hands of the bourgeoisie; furthermore, that he became more or less isolated from the bourgeoisie in the latter days of his life, because his idealism did in the post-independence years become a hindrance to the self-interest of the bourgeoisie.

Gandhism After Gandhi

Now that we have come to the end of the story of the life of Mohandas Karamchand Gandhi, the question naturally arises: where does the Gandhian school of thought stand today, nearly 10 years after its founder met with the tragic end at the hands of an assassin?

It is very interesting, in this connection, that, though many of the close followers and colleagues of Gandhi who are alive today, were once reputed to be the chief exponents of the Gandhian philosophy, they do not agree among themselves on the essence of Gandhism and its application to the complex problems of day-to-day life. As it was noted in the beginning of this book, there are several followers and disciples of Gandhi, each of whom claiming to be loyally following his teachings while criticizing others for betraying the ideals for which Gandhi spent a whole lifetime.

It is also interesting that, while several of the followers and disciples of Gandhi differ among themselves as to the essence of Gandhism and the manner of its application to present-day problems, one of them—Acharya Vinoba Bhave—is unanimously acclaimed as the true follower of the Mahatma, his real successor.

Vinoba Bhave was not known to the public as many others were during Gandhi's lifetime. The only occasion on which his name was broadcast throughout India as a loyal follower of Gandhi was in 1940 when Gandhi selected him as the first individual satyagrahi to break the law as a protest against Britain's forcing India into the war. People then came to know that he was a loyal and devoted follower of Gandhi, a silent and selfless worker in propagating and practising the ideals and principles for which Gandhi stood and fought.

It was only after more than a decade since this incident that his name again shot into prominence. The Bhoodan movement, which he initiated in 1951, was hailed as a true application of Gandhi's principles to the most important problem which free India has to solve—the problem of land. It was hailed as an alternative to the more painful method of forcing the landlords to part with their land and distributing it to the peasants. It did not matter whether this process of forcing the landlords was to be done through the constitutional means of enacting legislations as the Congress governments proposed to do, or through the militant mass peasant action as the Communists sought to do in Telangana. Just as in the case of Gandhi, so in the case of Vinoba Bhave too, it so happened that dozens of men and women who towered above him in intellectual capacity and other ingredients of personal eminence went to him, listened to his exposition of the gospel of Jan Shakti (people's power) as the only effective means through which land and other problems of the people can be solved. Ministers, professors and other eminent men began to hail him as the leader of a movement which, if successful, will lead to the realization of the goal for which they have all been working—the goal of establishing a classless and casteless society through non-violent means.

Barring this agreement in the matter of recognizing Vinoba Bhave as the true follower of their departed leader, there is no point on which one follower of the Gandhian school of the present day agrees with another. Take, for example, their attitude to the world problems of the present day. There are, among the present-day Gandhians, people who hold different views—ranging from those who are considered 'fellow-travelers' and 'crypto-Communists,' to those who would, at least in private, repeat almost everything that the notorious anti-Communists of the world have to say on the 'danger of communism.' On the problems of internal economy and politics too, there are all manner of views held by those who call themselves Gandhians, many of them being members and leaders of different political parties. On the other hand, there are some who had opposed Gandhi when he was heading the anti-imperialist movement, but who today claim themselves to be his followers, and what is worse, denounce many of the earlier followers of Gandhi for their 'non-adherence to Gandhian principles'!

The question arises: Why all this confusion within the Gandhian school? Why is it that the followers of Gandhi are fighting among themselves? Is it a case of history repeating itself: a prophet being able to keep his disciples united during his lifetime, but after his death, they falling out among themselves? If so, how is it that they are united in paying tribute to one of them (Vinoba Bhave) as the true follower and successor of the Mahatma? Again, why is it that, at the very time when the disciples of the Mahatma are fighting among themselves on the right way to apply his teachings to the present-day problems, many of those who were opposing him during his struggle against imperialism are today swearing by his name and claim to follow him?

For an answer to these questions, it is necessary to understand what is the essence of Gandhism. The answer usually given is that the essence of Gandhism consists in the application of the moral principles of truth and non-violence to the current problems of society. This would, of course, be a correct answer, but it would immediately raise another question: Is there some thing like absolute truth or absolute morality; are there unalterable ways of applying this absolute truth and absolute morality to the current problems of life? For example, how is it that Gandhi did not only fail to denounce participation in the First World War as a sin, but did himself actively participate in it on the side of the British by going about in his own Gujarat province recruiting soldiers for the British; while, during the Second World War, he considered it a sin not to dissociate oneself in all possible ways from the war? How is it that what was moral in the First World War became immoral in the Second? Again, how is it that the very Gandhi, who in 1921 denounced the government as 'Satanic' and called for the boycott of legislatures in 1921, subsequently used his personal influence with his 'no-change' followers to allow the Swarajists to function through the legislatures? How is it that

Gandhi, who ordered the withdrawal of civil disobedience and other forms of mass action when mass violence broke out in Chauri-Chaura, had no hesitation in giving support to the Congress government (in the provinces) who resorted to shooting of the masses? Is there anything like absolute morality, absolute truth, absolute non-violence, etc., in all these mutually contradictory positions taken by him?

These are questions which have been posed at various places in the previous pages. Now that we have come to the end of the story, we may sum up the discussion as a whole and state that, just as for any other human being, for Gandhi too, truth, morality and non-violence were not absolute but relative. He judged everything by the acid test of whether a particular course will help what was, in the larger interests, true and moral—the ending of British imperialism by peaceful and non-violent means.

Recruiting Indian soldiers for British imperialism was moral in the First World War, because, as he himself stated at the time, the personal sacrifice of Indian soldiers in defence of the British Empire would strengthen him and other fighters of self-government within that Empire. On the other hand, participation in the Second World War was immoral, because the threat of struggle against the war effort was, in the changed circumstances, the best means of strengthening the struggle for independence. Interestingly enough, Gandhi allowed the Congress, during certain phases of the movement, to negotiate with the British on the basis of participation in the war, though he personally abstained from participation; even this personal abstention was part of the strategy of keeping himself free, if later on the situation demanded it, to launch a struggle against the British.

So was the position with regard to his attitude to the 'Satanic' government and its legislative and other organs. Gandhi worked in 1921 for a mass boycott of the administrative organs of the government, but subsequently proved himself skilful in the negotiations with the Viceroy and other high officials.

It would, therefore, be dishonest for anybody to say that

Gandhi was sticking to absolute truth and absolute morality; equally dishonest will it be for anyone to claim that the followers and colleagues of Gandhi were absolutely loyal to all that Gandhi himself preached and tried to practise. On the other hand, there are ever so many of his colleagues and followers who, in private talks, used to make run of what are called 'Gandhi's fads.' The well-known discussion as to whether non-violence was a creed or policy, and the stand taken by several of his followers that, while for Gandhi it was a creed, for themselves it was only a policy, illustrates the relative character of the loyalty of both Gandhi as well as his followers to the basic tenets of what is called 'Gandhism'. Gandhi's ability to unite them all arose out of the fact that he applied the principles of truth, morality, non-violence, etc., to the needs of the anti-imperialist struggle as it was conceived by the class that was leading that struggle during his life time—the bourgeoisie. That class appreciated his skill in unleashing the mass of the toiling people and uniting them against the British, as well as in restricting the activity of these masses within the limits that are safe for the bourgeoisie. As the tide of anti-imperialist struggle followed its successive ebbs and flows, Gandhi felt the pulse of the people, kept contact with the British, and used his contact with both to keep the fire of anti-imperialism alive among the people. At the same time, he took care to see that the fire did not devour those who were afraid that their own interests will suffer if the common people came into their own. It was precisely because of this particular manner of Gandhi's application of the principles of truth, non-violence and morality that the true representatives of the bourgeoisie hailed him as their leader, though they had their own reservation with regard to the principles he preached.

The basic change that took place in the situation in August 1947 made it unnecessary for such an approach to problems. A gulf, therefore, appeared between Gandhi on the one hand and most of his colleagues on the other. His colleagues felt that, since state power had come into their hands, there was no necessity for any mass movement; on the other hand, mass movements might become a positive hindrance to them. Whatever reforms the socio-economic system required could be made through the use of state power. Gandhi, however, was not so hopeful. As has been explained in the preceding chapter, he was stricken with grief at the new developments that were taking place on the eve of, and after, the transfer of power. He thought it necessary to reformulate his principles to meet the altered situation. It was out of this realization on his part that his well-known proposals regarding the shape of things to come in free India emerged. He proposed that the Congress should be formed into a non-political organization—Lok Sahayak Sangh—which will exclusively devote itself to the service of the people.

This idea of transforming the Congress into a non-political organization was rejected by the leaders of the Congress. It appeared ridiculous to them that an organization which had fought for several decades for securing political power should deprive itself of the opportunity to use the newly-won political power in the interests of national development. They, therefore, set before themselves the programme of utilizing the state machinery that came into their hands on 15 August 1947 to reconstruct India on the lines which appealed to them.

Gandhi's idea, however, was taken up by a very small group of his closest followers and disciples working in the name of Sarva Seva Sangh. They took the pledge that they would not aspire for any position of power in the new political set-up: offices of ministers, MPs, MLAs, etc., were foreign to them; they would devote themselves to the service of the people through the same constructive programme which Gandhi had evolved during his lifetime, with such modifications as they thought necessary under the altered circumstances—khadi, village industries, basic education, etc. In other words, they functioned the Sarva Seva Sangh in the same way in which Gandhi wanted the Congress to function in the post-independence era.

It was out of these activities of the Sarvodaya workers, led by Acharya Vinoba Bhave, that a new movement was initiated—the movement of Bhoodan. The circumstances in which this movement originated are well-known: the peasants of Telangana who had originally risen against the Nizam-*shahi* and who, in the course of the anti-Nizam struggle had put an end to landlords' rule and redistributed land, came up against the Congress regime which succeeded the Nizam-*shahi*. Violent clashes took place between the peasants who tried to retain the land which they had seized from the landlords, and the police who were employed in suppressing the peasants' revolt. Dozens were shot dead, hundreds were arrested and imprisoned, and other forms of terror were employed in the struggle.

It was these developments that set Acharya Vinoba Bhave thinking on how these sufferings of the people can be avoided. The solution that flowed out of this thinking is typically Gandhian. Rejecting the method of revolutionary seizure of land adopted by the peasants under Communist leadership, he also rejected the method of bringing about agrarian reforms through legislative measures adopted by the Congress government; in place of both these methods (each of which, in its own way, involved violence in the solution of social problems: while the first was mass action and thus involved direct violence, the second involved the use of the state machinery which, after all, is the use of organized force by the majority against the minority), he advocated the method of voluntary parting of the land by those who owned it. His well-known slogan of 'every man to part with one-sixth of his or her land for the landless' was an alternative both to the revolutionary seizure of land by the peasants, as well as to the constitutional method of imposing the will of the majority over the minority. Jan Shakti (people's power), as opposed to Raj Shakti (state power), for the solution of the land problem—this is the essence of Bhoodan.

It was this Bhoodan movement that went through various phases and became Gramdan. Bhave is no more satisfied with people surrendering one-sixth of their land as he was in the phase of Bhoodan, but want everybody to surrender his or her entire property. Abolition of private property (property in land to begin with); the pooling of the entire land property of a village into the common property of the village community, the common cultivation of all the village lands and equitable distribution of the produce of the land; organization of cottage industries and other means of livelihood in the common interest to the people of the village—such, in short, is the picture of the new villages visualized by Bhave when he speaks of Gramdan.

This, therefore, can correctly be called the application (to the main problems of the post-independence era in our country) of those very principles which Gandhi had applied to the problems of our country in the years of anti-imperialist struggle. The objective which Bhave placed before the people is as revolutionary as any socialist or Communist would have; it is that very basic principle, 'from each according to his ability, to each according to his needs,' which, according to the Marxists, can be applied only in the higher phase of socialism, or its communist phase. However, this objective has to be realized not through the prolonged process of political struggle by the working people under the leadership of the working class; transformation of the ruled majority of the oppressed and exploited classes into the ruling classes; establishment of the state power of the working people and through it the abolition of class distinctions; the development of the productive forces of society to such a stage that it will be possible, in actual practice, to realize the goal of 'to each according to his needs,' etc., but through persuasion and change of heart. This is the essence of Gramdan or Gandhism at its latest phase; and it is here that it differs from Marxism.

Bhave and his followers claim that they have discovered through this Gramdan movement, the only possible and correct solution for the social problems facing our country. This, however, is not conceded either by the Congress leaders or by such parties of the left as the Communist Party, the PSP, etc. While admitting that Bhave's preachings against the evils of private property in land and the necessity for the reorganization of the entire village life would help the process of socio-economic transformations, they point out that these transformations cannot be brought about except through the use of state machinery. Despite all the successes attained by Bhave and the Gramdan movement under his leadership, the fact remains that the big landlords do not respond to his call for the abolition of private property in land. That was why the Mysore conference of political leaders, convened by Bhave in order to discuss the Gramdan movement, made it perfectly clear that while the political leaders, belonging to different political parties, have full sympathy for this movement, they do not consider it as a substitute for governmental action by way of land reforms, organization of the cooperative movement, etc. It was agreed that the voluntary movement for socio-economic changes initiated by Bhave and governmental action are complementary to each other.

It is significant, in this connection, that the majority of the most eminent colleagues of Gandhi in his lifetime do not have that faith in the Gramdan movement as a panacea for the socio-economic ills of our country which Bhave and his colleagues have. The significance of this will be clear when it is seen that most of those who today have less faith in Jan Shakti, or people's power, and more faith in Raj Shakti, or state power, than Bhave and his colleagues have, were the very people who differed from Gandhi on various occasions and on various issues, such as the attitude to legislatures and elections, the attitude to participation in war, the programme of transforming the Congress into a non-political organization of service to people, etc. For, it means that their acceptance of Gandhi as their activities, was just a means to realize the end of political power. They accepted Gandhi's preachings of truth, non-violence, morality, etc., only because it helped them to realize their goal of political power. Today, too, they are not prepared to renounce political power and its use, since they feel, as hard-headed realists, that the success or failure of any movement for socio-economic change very much depends on who wields political power and how it is used.

As for the Communists, socialists and other leftists, it is clear to them that political power is an essential factor in the struggle for socio-economic transformations. As the founders of Marxism had declared a century ago, no class voluntarily renounces power; an individual here or an individual there may be roused by the noble preachings of a Bhave or some other idealist and renounce power and property; but the landlords, the capitalists, and other exploiting classes will not, as a class, willingly subject themselves to the social transformations dreamed of by visionaries and fought for by practical revolutionaries. They will, therefore, certainly wish Bhave and his colleagues well, do all that is within their power to help the propagation of the ideals of the Gramdan movement, but will never give up their struggle for political power.

Institutionalized

The last chapter was written over 23 years ago—in the latter half of 1957. Much has happened during this long period in the politics of the country in general, in the development of Gandhism as a theory and practice in particular.

We had left the story at a point when a small band of Gandhi followers were demarcating themselves from the mainstream of Gandhian politicians who were busy making full use of the newly-won opportunities to enrich themselves, their relatives and friends at the expense of the people. While the chief lieutenants of Gandhi in the days of the freedom struggle, those who were then known as his loyal followers, were running the Central and State Governments and fighting their group and factional battles all over the country, Vinoba Bhave and a small band around him were going from place to place, broadcasting the message of Bhoodan and Gramdan, etc. Hence the distinction between the Jan Shakti (people's power) and Raj Shakti (State power) underlined by Vinoba Bhave.

Gradually, however, this distinction between the Jan Shakti and the Raj Shakti started disappearing. Vinoba Bhave and a few others were of course not participants in the power game and therefore out of the ring in the scramble for political jobs. However, innumerable links came to be forged between this Jan Shakti and the Raj Shakti. The Sarvodaya movement, the various institutions and organizations which it represented, came to occupy a semi-official status. Furthermore, many who lost the battle for power in the States or at the Centre went to the Sarvodaya movement which became a haven for such people.

The Gandhi centenary organized on a countrywide scale in 1969, in fact, became for all practical purpose an officially-organized function. The President, the Prime Minister, her cabinet colleagues and their counterparts at the State, district and lower levels became the organizers of the centenary celebrations, 'ably assisted', of course, by the top and medium level bureaucrats. The official and semi-official activities prior to and connected with the centenary celebrations culminated in the setting up of enormous institutions, such as the Gandhi Peace Foundation at the Centre and Gandhi Smarak Nidhis at lower levels.

Having thus come very close to the Raj Shakti, those who talked of Jan Shakti became part of the Establishment, although formally out of any governmental office. They, therefore, could not help being thrown into the maelstrom of factional politics when the ruling party came to be split into two. Following this split, a liaison developed between a section of those who were in the ruling party before the split and a section of the opposition. Cutting the story short, we may just note that, by the middle of the 1970s, a section of the Sarvodayites started coming closer to the Opposition led by the Congress (O), Jan Sangh and Swatantra, while another stood by the ruling faction of the old undivided ruling party.

The reference here is to the pre-emergency months when Jayaprakash Narayan, who was considered next only to Vinoba Bhave in the top echelons of the Sarvodaya movement, took up the banner of revolt against the authoritarianism represented by Indira Gandhi. What is commonly known as the 'JP movement' caught the imagination of thousands of Sarvodayites. The movement led by him against authoritarianism, for electoral and educational reforms, against corruption, etc., became a new version of the Gandhi-led movements of 1921, 1930–32 and 1942—in the last of which Jayaprakash himself had played an outstanding role. The new JP movement was a new edition also of the Bhoodan and Gramdan movement initiated by Vinoba Bhave over a decade ago, of which JP became an active participant.

There was, however, one big difference between the Bhoodan and Gramdan movement initiated by Bhave and the 'JP movement' launched in the first half of the 1970s. The former was non-political in the sense that it had no demand on the government. It was a purely popular movement calculated to generate the Jan Shakti, though there was no conflict between it and the Raj Shakti. The 'JP movement' on the other hand, was directed, mainly and above all, against the Raj Shakti in its naked form. Hence the wide popular response which that movement evoked.

This was not to the liking of Vinoba Bhave and the band of Sarvodayites closely allied to him. They opposed the identification of the Sarvodaya movement with the anti-authoritarian political movement initiated by JP. The Sarvodaya movement thus got split into two.

This split in the Sarvodaya movement, with the topmost two leaders (Bhave and JP) on opposite sides should be seen against the background of the split that was taking place among the political representatives of the ruling classes. The 1969 split of the Congress party culminated in the emergence of what was called the 'grand alliance', uniting the Congress group that went into the opposition and other bourgeois opposition parties. The Socialists who were in the Opposition also joined this alliance. The section of the Sarvodayites led by JP were at one with this 'grand alliance', while those led by Vinoba Bhave stood firmly with the Establishment.

This division continued in the Emergency and post-Emergency period too. Vinoba Bhave acted as the high priest of the authoritarian Indira Congress, while the tallest two of the other Sarvodaya wing—Kripalani and Jayaprakash—acted as the godfathers of the Janata opposition. The division between the pro- and anti-authoritarian wings of the political representatives of the bourgeois-landlord ruling classes, in other words, found reflection in the Sarvodaya movement as well.

This metamorphosis of what was originally called Jan Shakti into the aid and support of two forms of Raj Shakti further confirms the view expressed in the preceding pages that Gandhism is the theory and practice of bourgeois politics. It acted in the period of freedom struggle as the instrument in the hands of the bourgeoisie for mobilizing as well as containing the militant anti-imperialism of the people. In the period of the crisis which erupted on the eve of and following the attainment of Independence, a hiatus came into the open between Gandhi and his chief lieutenants. This was to a certain extent bridged when the Bhoodan-Gramdan movement initiated by Vinoba Bhave sought to generate Jan Shakti. This Jan Shakti however gradually got institutionalized into a prop and support of the Raj Shakti. Naturally therefore, when the Raj Shakti got split, the Gandhian movement too split. This is the fate that overtook the social outlook which, shorn of its idealistic appearance, is in fact the theory and practice of the growing bourgeois class.

In assessing Gandhism, therefore, Marxists-Leninists should take into account both the positive as well as the negative features of the philosophy and practice of the bourgeoisie as a class. Whether against imperialism as in the days fo the freedom struggle, or against feudal landlordism as in the Bhoodan movement, or against authoritarianism as in the 1970s, Gandhism championed the cause of national freedom, agrarian reforms and defence of democracy respectively. At the same time, with its revivalist and obscurantist socio-cultural outlook, this same philosophy became an impediment in the unfettered development of mass initiative.

This latter aspect was seen in the latest phase when the Sarvodaya leaders split into the pro- and anti-authoritarian wings but both joined in raising the question of ban on cow-slaughter. Though the Vinoba Bhave faction used this question against the Morarji-led Janata Government, the other faction of the Sarvodayites too joined in the demand and gave him support.

Marxist-Leninists, therefore, should carry on a principled, ideological struggle against the philosophy and practice of Gandhism, though, on specific issues where it is possible to develop joint actions, the opportunity should be fully utilized.

Index

Also from LeftWord

The Frontline Years

Selected Articles

E.M.S. Namboodiripad

978-81-87496-93-9, paperback, pp. 275

E.M.S. Namboodiripad is perhaps modern India's most important Marxist theoretician.

From 1991 till his death in 1998, EMS wrote a column in the newsmagazine *Frontline*. The present volume puts together a selection of his *Frontline* columns. This volume is a testimony to the variety of his interests, his erudition, and his ability to communicate complex questions of history and theory in simple and elegant prose. EMS discusses, among other things, the roles and contributions of Congress leaders from Dadabhai Naoroji and Ranade to Gandhi, Subhas Bose and Nehru to Narasimha Rao and Manmohan Singh; he discusses the thoughts and relevance of Marxist theoreticians including Engels, Lenin, Rosa Luxemburg, Mao Zedong, Stalin and Deng Xioping, as well as Nelson Mandela; he writes on religion, philosophy and art; he discusses important questions of the Indian polity including planning, decentralization and centre-state relations; he comments on the Indian Communist movement (including on the decision not to join the United Front government at the centre in 1996); and he writes about the radical experiments in Kerala.

Also from LeftWord

History, Society and Land Relations

Selected Essays

E.M.S. Namboodiripad

978-81-87496-92-2, paperback, pp. 240

E.M.S. Namboodiripad is perhaps modern India's most important Marxist theoretician.

The present volume puts together his essays spanning six decades, from 1937 to 1996. Included in the volume are classic essays such as 'The Question of Land Tenure in Malabar', 'A Short History of the Peasant Movement in Kerala', 'Caste Conflict versus Growing Unity of Popular Democratic Forces', 'Marxism, Leninism and Bourgeois Judiciary', 'Adi Shankara and his Philosophy: A Marxist View', 'The Class Character of the Nineteenth Century Renaissance in India' and 'The Marxist Theory of Ground Rent: Relevance to the Study of the Agrarian Question in India'.

LeftWord Books
2254/2A Shadi Khampur
New Ranjit Nagar
New Delhi 110008
INDIA
www.leftword.com